Furniture Music

Furniture

Gail Scott

Wave Books
Seattle/
New York

Music

A Northern in Manhattan: Poets/Politics [2008–2012]

Published by Wave Books

www.wavepoetry.com

Copyright © 2023 by Gail Scott

Wave Books titles are distributed to the trade by

Consortium Book Sales and Distribution

Phone: 800-283-3572 / SAN 631-760x

Library of Congress Cataloging-in-Publication Data

Names: Scott, Gail, 1945– author.

Title: Furniture music : a Northern in Manhattan: poets/politics [2008–2012] / Gail Scott.

Description: First edition. | Seattle : Wave Books, [2023]

Identifiers: LCCN 2023009905 | ISBN 9781950268863 (paperback)

Subjects: LCSH: Scott, Gail, 1945- —Homes and haunts—New York (State)—New York. |
    Scott, Gail, 1945- —Friends and associates. | Scott, Gail, 1945- —Political and social views. |
    Authors, Canadian—20th century—Biography. | Politics and literature—United States—
    History—21st century. | LCGFT: Autobiographies

Classification: LCC PR9199.3.S35 Z46 2023 | DDC 818/.5408—dc23/eng/20230321

LC record available at https://lccn.loc.gov/2023009905

Designed by Crisis

Printed in the United States of America

9 8 7 6 5 4 3 2 1

First Edition

2008

BOOKS TOO NEED THEIR DAY OF REST
THIS PREFACE IS OUR SUNDAY

Why . . . still wanting to say 'Bolshevik?'

If, as is commonly held, life supplies biography—the Bolsheviks, in
extremis, sought *to control biography by organizing every aspect of life.
Without grasping* THE ANARCHY OF LIFE.

Viktor
Shklovsky

*You, well-bathed in your late 20th potpourri of proto-Marxism/
psychoanalysis/linguistics/queer/avant art, were happy to go with* that!
*Easily holding language as primary in shaping occurrence. Only. You
felt wary of sentencing's promiscuous tilt toward the preconfigured or
habitual. Were not poetry's slants, estrangements, apostrophes better
suited in current iterative, automatic-reflex media context to address
the unreliability of predicates to do with time? Had we not seen it all*
before? *Money markets falling after rapacious accumulation to
ever-insurgent sound of war. While top one per cent holding more
than half entire nation's wealth. For your ramble between two sites
[Montréal/Manhattan], two [or more] elections, a Krasch + apparent
'recovery,' best engage the poets. . . . . Mercifully, a poet is any* ONE:

Harlem, 2008. Soft snow falling. Obama just elected.

Man on sidewalk calling out white family passing:

> No more White
>
> In the White House
>
> Black Pres-i-DENT

Street Vendor

> In The Res-i-DENCE.........

Or was Time ... merely apostrophized a minute? ... A-woke +
crowding after tall narrow suit running toward The Residence. Behind,
running woman candidate in blue electric pantsuit, thought ugly by the
media. You were well conversed in the irony of that. Not to mention
background stock market hitting bottom. [Shortly to be rescued by Fed.]
Behind Greek-revival columns. To Hellenic chorus of millions of housing
bubble mortgage foreclosees. Soon to be advised: If your home was
foreclosed between 2008 + 2011, claim forms will be mailed to you.
If you think you may be hard to locate [living in your car?], you
can file a claim with your state attorney general. *Along SoHo streets*
near your temporary Québec Arts Council studio. Scrubbed, pressed,
anxious, newly unemployed, patient, maybe even hungry, lining double
round entire block for one single job. Pathetic. To want to throw a brick
through a window.

Any account of another country is an account of one left behind. Satie
called background music FURNITURE MUSIC. *Trotting up Bowery,*
under Obama campaign portrait-posters. Somewhere between Che style
socialist + American super-hero in design. FURNITURE MUSIC's *playing*

pale-eyed right-wing robot-haircut cozy of North's Bitumen Family
Compact. *Soon to be re-elected on promise of transparency. Ere* Stephen
Harper
*proroguing Parliament, once, twice, thrice. Walking over tundra-like
landscape. Wife Laureen in white bell-bottom pantsuit holding his hand.
He seeming distant, parodic. Next elegant Obama. Wooing war-+-
economy-weary ever more elated audiences. With liberal striped-with-
vernacular rhetoric. Young woman on YouTube, stilettos, ultra-tight
short-shorts, pole-dancing on bus pole. Lip-synching* I got a crush on
Obama.

Or could one say, Time as palindrome, almost? The initial **2008**
*euphoria surrounding Barack Obama. Who in Time's next pirouette to
have been running again. Blown like Klee's angel into future. Head bent
back against deluge of cumulating hostility. As if so many. Electoral
campaign after electoral campaign. Running toward perpetually
promised, unfulfillable-to-point-of-running-backwards . . . HOPE. For
we commonly conceive our words as capturing what we will have been
[in time] . . . yet the future perfect [so hopefully alluded] remains
irreducible to this economy. New York poet admonishing*: Jacques Derrida

Never did I receive your

Public lettering Marjorie Welish

*Your essayist, herein, with her biographer-weakness for psychology. [Is
not the reader comforted by psychology?]. May be, with her sentencing,
fixed in a* PERIOD*-izing frame. Yet, with the poet, also desiring a present.
Whose end cannot be seen. Wanting perhaps narrative that contains*

non-narrative. Not to be dispensing history's authoritarian insistence on idées reçues. *Sponsored by ever more transactional public discourse.* *To wit, media coverage of Obama: That* [**2008**] natural politician with skills to burn ... has ... conquered his identity issues, ... an inspirational figure who obviously loves his country + may just ... transform parts of it ... *Then thoroughly* [**2012**] *excoriated by [formerly] besotted opinionator. From iconic liberal paper ... As* cool cat ... who connected so electrically and facilely, ... causing Americans to overlook his thin résumé, cannot seem to connect anymore. *Another voice opining*: The President held to higher standards than white counterparts—to point of leading an army amassed against him ... *Indeed* ... narrative is out there somewhere—but it is processed into structure before it can appear.

Best then, as Northern visiting America, but inhabiting French-America. In another country not named America. To be focussing, in this early [**2008–12**] *Obama era. On what hidden in notion of word* Citizen. *As informed by poet-acquaintances of downtown Manhattan, Brooklyn. Next others from North of 49th. Where* concept *meaning something else entirely. Starting with old reprobate Gertrude Stein. Who, like our Northern, also writing in English. In a French-speaking place. The American, in Paris. Writing estrangingly, yet, somehow, also biographically. Over gaps between languages, over solipsism's time-locked opinions. Declaring re: time [history] in portrait of Picasso:*

As or as presently
Let me recite what history teaches. History teaches..........

Ruben Navarrette Jr.

Maureen Dowd

Charles Blow

Joshua Clover

Gertrude Stein

Revealing, by writing "presently" [meaning sometimes now; sometimes little later]. Language's inevitable ambivalence re: time. Further suggesting history is, fundamentally, homily. Or iteration. I.e., idée reçue! *Yet, in immediately repeating the phrase* history teaches. *Implying [psychology again] history at least somewhat teaches.*

THE SHIP OF CITIZEN

Friend R—trope in this tale for born + bred New Yorker—writing: *The State or me / or if I am the State. // I am a collection / of desire // precariously / housed.*

Rachel Levitsky

You would not have said you are the State. Even precariously housed. Your belle province [Québec] being less a ship of Citizens than one of several boats bobbing. But nor could you. Sitting, at end of 4-year Montréal↔Manhattan ambit. On modular sofa of faux-deco New York West Village flat. Watching 2nd Obama Presidential election. Quite echo Canadian soprano Teresa Stratas's tremulous Kurt Weil scored "A stranger here myself." For if not being one of an ... *AMERICA* ... *BIGGER THAN THE SUM OF OUR INDIVIDUAL AMBITIONS.* Still feeling a-part of tearful Chicago television audience. Ecstatic at President Obama's repeat rout of white-bread Republicans. A black man twice elected NOT, after all, just the movies. Someone quipping *Black man gets country's worst job. . . .*

Kurt Weill

Barack Obama

[Here, FURNITURE MUSIC. In back of head. Striking up refrain. *Ostinato.* Of North country's tragic historic divide. As group of youthful First Nations. Fastest growing Canadian youth demographic. Setting out from James Bay on snowshoes. Headed for Parliament. *We are losing our territories, without them we are nothing.* Walking for days. In up to −40C weather. Joined by hundreds more. Bearing gift for Conservative Canadian Prime Minister: Pair of beautifully crafted snowshoes. But where is Mr. Harper on day they arriving in Ottawa capital? In another city welcoming pair of pandas. Flown in from China. *They're very wriggly*, he giggles.]

And poetry, in relation to above? How might enjambments, chronic interruptions, spatial [body] logic [wanting *to paw the world, not see*]. Be offering better map for Citizen digression from tired templates. Than narration's purposeful aspirations? Are poetry's tergiversations philosophical? Arcane mirrors? A *Recalculating*? Or *Annotations* to the present? Perhaps nexus of engagement? Conversational like lines on a placard? *Someone says general strike/now there is a good idea.* And if poetry is language's DNA [as poets priding to claim]. To what good purpose may one be putting writing in sentences?

Charles Baudelaire

Charles Bernstein
John Keene
Levitsky

Your prosaist's cheap saddle shoes—splaying flesh-pink faux-rubber soles. One more shopping error in Manhattan. To appear cool, gender neutral. Is not fashion reflecting epoch? Crinoline in time of Imperialist expansion. "Sadistic" bloomers for era of suffragettes. Now post-Krasch silhouette narrow, dark, stark.

Limping down **2012** leafy West-side street. Smelling of rain-soaked Chelsea posies. Toward more edgy [summer girl in dumpster-style pink faux fur hat with giant flaps despite 30C thermometer, skimpy summer dress, riding her bike] East Village. In pocket, poem by lovely Dada-inflected downtown poet. Her skinny lines. Parodying troop-entertainers performing *nothing, [i.e., memory-avoidance for mutilators fresh from the charge]*. Lines laughing like tears down a snout:

to go

overseas

we had to

get

vaccinated

as good as

they gave me

the

shot

for

Anthrax

now we

can

eat

unconcerned

at

any

given

Taco / B. . . . . . .   Kim Rosenfield

Too bad poetic language making people nervous. Are not prose's suppositions, comparisons, descripts, more clarifying? Haltingly you trot. Toward Ave of Americas. Stuck tight with yellow cabs, 6 abreast. Clients treating every moment as if it were the ultimate. Ordaining your retreat. Back to comfy West-side liberal nest. Eye on shop windows for bargains to achieve post-Krasch silhouette: Grey, black + narrow. Implying want + social friction. Then eating sausage + polenta. Prunes in creamy mascarpone. Scratchy Dylan tune emitting from 8th St speaker. Near diner, where older residents still calling selves The Villagers. Shaggy hair + collars. Bent over well-greased *Bonbonniere* breakfast. Outside diner window, sleek young professionals gunning weekend strollers. Several white + staring. When one night you pausing there so poet companion, black. Can stow her wallet in your backpack.

"They think I'm robbing you."

Perhaps poetry's dérives at best. Offering. Like cutting-edge inventions. Rampart against general failure to imagine. Take that North poet behind a door. Alberta Rockies shining in background. Gliding, there, high above direct social issues/lower sensibilities. In favour [no less]. Of transforming computer science, physics. Back to earthy matter. . . . *I have been striving to write a short verse about language and genetics,* then using a *"chemical alphabet" to translate* ... *into a sequence of DNA for subsequent* implantation into the genome of a bacterium. ... Potential act of beauty. Lauding a critic. You balking at endgame of "beauty." In aiming for beauty—is not one risking *indifference.* . . . *for all that lies outside the object contemplated*? Plus—work operating on cusp of new meaning. Oft seen as *irritating annoying stimulating then all quality of beauty* ... *denied to it.* STILL—

Christian Bök

Theodor Adorno

Stein

. . . .*Litter gravitates toward the spaced*

Creases   the imbricated spacing yet it distributes differently

Think of epochs and historical formations

Of courtyards:

Welish

IS BEAUTIFUL. And R shouting on phone. In ironic okay-to-be-greedy way. "When I see beauty I WANT it!" Was not your dear WB [you maybe quoting too much]. Also torn between raggedly idealistic avant-thinking. And perpetual need for classic harmony of proportion? Warning of beautiful semblance's tendency to reify past. In history's index of nostalgia. [*Like a bad* (bourgeois) *poem about spring.*] Proposing, rather, to wrench life + life's artifacts. From time-worn normalizing contexts. Such as occurring in revolutionary disruption. Where, in heat of struggle. Past/present/future colliding. In flash of collective awareness Surrealists calling *profane illumination.* B also deploying—for purpose of self-estrangement. Divine hashish dream walks in pre-war Marseilles. Above all, he collecting found objects.

Walter Benjamin

Dusty texts, old ads, newspaper anecdotes ancient or contemporaneously marginal, fragmented tableaux of Paris gardens, worker uprisings, dolls, city planning. Items, torn from historicism's forward march. And reassembled in disjunct critical constellations. To *rub history against the grain.*

Benjamin

What devil here making you think of Michelle Obama's arms? Torn repeatedly during first [**2008**] Obama campaign. From context of her person. And singled out as THING of unrivaled beauty?? An article of consumption: . . . "*[Arms that] many women would part with their firstborn to have.*" . . . . "*The Secret behind Michelle Obama's arms finally revealed.*" . . . . "*She's made her point —now she should put away thunder + lightning.*" *BABE!* [Republican Senator].

Yes, and the body has memory. . . . is the threshold across which each objectionable call passes into consciousness. That is—speech! Which is infinitive. Ideally unspooling along a line of intrinsic/extrinsic. In ways allowing one to be safely contiguous with others.

Claudia
Rankine

PSYCHOLOGY, WITH ORGANS
[OUR PROSAIST, INELUCTABLY, BEGINS]

... Deplaning one sky-blue July [2008] day. LaGuardia. Gail's car service's sailing through clear blue air. Bloating with writerly intentions. Bloating even more in slow elevator [scattered take-out Asian resto pamphlets]. Then steel-frame door. Swinging open onto wide white columned space. Really—yours? Six whole months? Ambition rising to boiling. The canny [post]-colonized Québécois. Knowing an artist needing ego to produce. Friend R already deep in black leather sofa. With Euro-French beau. Himself, laughing at studio coffee table's incongruous curled brass animal feet. "Likely recycled from some embassy." Gail [sotto voce]:

"... Québec not a country."

Studio has 4 large square windows. Two filled with creaky air conditioners. [Alas, sash's stuck. Enhancing plastic odour from furniture store under.] And nice rosy dusk. Painting corner of exposed whitewashed brick wall. Auspicious halo, also backlighting muscled window washer. Rising on pulley. R, being expedient New Yorker. Knowing to grasp an opportunity. Noting social order's ... *rules against certain pleasures and extensive systems of reporting, ... now inside our buildings ... socializing, having coffee, smoking pot, giving advice to our neighbors. We know many of us have tried him, the window washer, the service of his love.* Now saying maybe wanting to stay night. Peering into crisp blue-+-white accessorized guestroom. Spider-tattooed curve of neck. Rapidly assembling/reassembling. But

Levitsky

Round midnight. Laying back. Solo. On crisp box-patterned sheets. Imbibing *that...drug—ourselves—...we take in solitude.* On TV screen, US flag big as football field. Patriots making indeterminate Fourth of July noise. News loop of mortgage-foreclosed houses. Bent or broken cheap construction materials. Going for price of groceries, almost. Exterminator ad's yellow bedbug nymphs amassing in walls. Ah, here's some HOPE. Pharmaceutical erection-enhancement. If hard-on persisting more than 4 hours—go to emergency. You laugh. Then Horatio on *CSI Miami*, Marlboro-man cop, racing not on horse. But swamp buggy o'er Everglade horizon. Red hair flying. Glancing down a second. Manly expression of ready to unzip. You love the flat language of police reports. Late into night, past pale Wooster façades, industrious feet pushing carts instead of barrows. Almost Dickensian.

Benjamin

WHEN DID MODERNITY PERISH?

CEASE?

CEASE AND DESIST? ....

Welish

On cue—revival Batman-Joker. Poster boy for villainous resistance. To stifling symbolic-order laws, institutions, ethics + values, so overwhelming, in order to destroy we destroying ourselves. Entering via stuck-shut window. Which fellow

Commonwealthian freshly dead from insomnia [pills]. Just down block. Sitting companionably on bed. Fan whirring over. Together you listening to raucous 3 am grinding of huge garbage trucks nosing like mammoth cockroaches down Wooster St cobblestones in waves. He steps into your head. Sleepless a week! It was the combined effects of oxycodone, hydrocodone, diazepam, temazepam, alprazolam, + doxylamine that killed your fellow-Commonwealthian. Insomnia [he saying] = loneliness. Plastic martini glass on kitchen counter. Holding welcome cocktail of drugs.

5:30a [90°!]: On TV, wide-screen Obama. Slim suit, shades. And Michelle. Stylish in her American way. Legs, lean, gorgeously dressed. Late 50s, your Mother in her little hat. Whose daughter's red eye spying. On African woman artist asleep. Behind sole open Wooster window sans ubiquitous AC unit. On wall, portrait of O. Off to replay historic JFK *Ich-bin-ein-Berliner*, by Brandenburg Gate. Till fastidious Germans nixing premature *We're-next-Camelot* projection. Obliging adoring Berliners to be rushing *en masse*. To cheer President's rock-star charisma at less iconic Victory Column. Some asshole venting in CNN commentary box:

CNN and Un-american media!!! I click on a story about McCain and get that socialist raceis (sic), *muslem POS obama, too bad the plane accident had a positive outcome* ☹. *God, . . . if that half bread wins!!!. . . .*

But . . . the Heat! Day after day. Making dogs go mad. *And citadins.* Hunkering in AC'd boxes. Succumbing to *frénésies.* Fevers. Or just Time's redux corridor. Eternally winding back to noontime CSI Horatio. Prancing in swamp vehicle over wetland. Red hair blowing to side. Surely, you telling R on phone [kindly, not laughing]. This being contemporary mirror of old film noir. High-toned as if painted. Underlying evil = Blonde Calleigh. Mounting gorgeous bi-racial Eric. She 'accidentally' shooting. Only when sunset again rosy. On fretted Wooster lintels. Is your own fresh-showered *beau-véhicule/mauvaise-pilote.* Looping into clammy SoHo eve. Past small French Dior window. Nipples staring misty. Through translucent undergarment tissue. And Apple Palace masses. Jostling for iPhone 3G's countless new features, apps, fastest touchscreen keyboard ever. And Gucci bags. And modernist Scandinave jewelry/fabric. No poet print nor scat anywhere discernible. Trotting toward Hudson. Through filth + the factories. Sultry, the smell of sulphur. Writing: *River smelt good, but up close brown, thick + litter. Someone kayaking through detritus.* . . .Ach! too Earnest-Canadian. Pedantic. Compared to, say, Lower East Side poet's nervy kayak-metronome:

. . . after wilderness comes the white bridge   closed off at third avenue

the neighborhood divides onto second avenue and then onto first   river

drive at night and is never dark   kayakers paddle softly about tugboats and

giant

cruise ships several stories high as they pass apartment building windows of

concrete blocks . . .

. . . the sun moves closer to its zenith, and

heats the skyscraper peaks. They melt, and a small wiggle distorts the clouds

behind them. Plastic slides down a measurement at a time and joins with

the metal substructures beneath it.

Marcella
Durand

R adumbrating: "The more staying in. The more autobiographical the writing." Thus, to West Broadway. Straggling by store doors, wide open. Cold AC air entropying out. To be sucking sweltering Citizens in. Gail puking in gutter. Ex-beau last night. Having come 'to rescue.' She exiting claustro box-metal subway elevator. Into greeny Brooklyn Heights. Loving the nicely cooling breeze. Coming from water. Air almost *sans* sooty particles. And classy high-rise apartment view. Over bay. Over gaping hole where Twin Towers stood. Your ex, old lefty. Now in finance. Not worried re: Krasch. [*Maybe* having to fire some friends.] Pretty wife, reviewed in the *Times*. Watching Gail. Nervously downing entire bottle of red [they only drinking white]. Poisonous in heat. At door, wagging tail in gratitude. "You better go with her for taxi." Nauseous a week. Still no poets.

That Parisian COMMIE ... [your inner Bolshie whispering]:
Jean-Paul Sartre. In deplaning [**1945**] from other great Republic.
To breathe American air of freedom. Likewise failing to grasp
city's abstruse symbolics. Complaining to Simone: 1) American
girlfriend too energetic. 2) White Manhattan skies, forested with
Capital's frenetically sprouting high-rises, making him feel
nobody. While Camus [the better writer]. Regaling in noise,
colours, smells, taxis, tie shops, ice cream, Giant Camel icon ad of
soldier, *mouth open, puffing clouds of real smoke*. His favourite [is not   Andy Martin
his own novel starting: *Mother died today* ... ?]: A funeral parlor   Albert Camus
ad. "You die. We do the rest." But one thing materialist Sartre
getting better. Island city, in trying to fortify against nature,
letting nature in on every side. Snow, heat, wind, rain. . . .

No. *Not* rain. Only plink plink of leaky upper floor AC on own
metal window unit. Bringing up manager of Happy Nesting
Furniture Store. Saying you dripping on her entrance. Driving off
business. Implied litigation. At window you pointing up to where
drip coming from floor above. Down below. Stopping taxi with
Mummy [the movie] ad on top. Little girl draping expensive dress.
Over well-primped Daddy. What scent prosperity to be thus
bewitching princess daughter? R saying good families presenting
like angels. With stardust on them. [FURNITURE MUSIC'S
playing **1970**s liberal elementary school somewhere in Montréal.
Overwhelmingly single-parent population: mullets, bad jeans,

torn lace, fat ladies smoking with high-toned anxiety. Common to former lefties + romantics]. Now

Your lumpy jeans. Dubbed weekend by NY fashionistas. Being careful not to pause. On SoHo Broadway corner. Lest rushy pushy mass knocking into traffic. Or *ballottant* toward pickpocketers. *You meaning* [admonishing inner Bolshie] *IMPECUNIOUS EXILES*! Leaning in doorways. Watching sun shine between buildings. Musing, as in song. How on Broadway to lure a girl. Without a dime. To offer—ok, not glitter. But if ain't had enough to eat: Dean + DeLuca almond Danish, roast beef tartine, seared yellowfin tuna/mango chutney. High on building: Obama poster. *HOPE* writ huge along bottom. No sign of female Democrat leader aspirant. "Shoulder-pad Hillary." About whom *Times* commentator sniding: ... *Hillary ... can't be superior to Obama in international crisis management because ... she's only done domestic crisis management, cleaning up after Frisky Bill! Is the message she is ready on Night One? That she won't have to waste any time if she's routed out of bed in the wee hours, because she's wearing a pantsuit*
Dowd   *under her pantsuit.*

Indeed, right pair of jeans. Making taller, sexier. Dare one say —happier? USians being people capable of emitting a particular we're-in-this-together. That jeans represent. Forthright as wide roads cutting straight across horizons. Or campaign speeches where every class 'the middle.' [Every family, nuclear.] *"Why?"*

you asking lefty novelist sitting in Kelly + Ping. Eating tofu wrap + dumplings. [You loving authentic undussied import warehouse ambience. Giant ceiling fans, pressed-metal roof, dark wood tables, box shelves covering walls lined with large jars of tea, hoisin, etc. Turning out to be citational.] *"Why*, in speaking of class, is Obama hardly saying 'working-?'" Novelist, brown sweater/brown cords [a realist], replying. Impatient: "To feel middle's to be a part of it." Gail, sipping Oolong Ginseng + sweating. Throwing back head, eyes closed. Laughing, in fake-sheepish way of suggesting North's multi-party system allowing for more nuanced class discourse. [Sort of.]

Another foreigner—Brazilian—similarly querying leading NY bard: *What* [are] . . . *Barack Obama's plans . . . What does change mean? . . . Does he have content? How do you refute the Republican line that he is a celebrity and not a politician with ideas? It's not that I think this* [sic] *but I have listened in São Paulo to upper middle class people say that he is a fool! . . . the black people from Rio's favelas love Obama, their new hero. They call him "O bamba"—homophonic translation of Obama, that means in slang tough guy, bully, hood—the best, the one . . . from samba, from Nigeria Bantu I think.* Oh oh! Is it those Obama-denigrating upper-middle-class Brazilians doing slinky samba in head? As if: *That you, Babe??* Non. NON!!! True, you intimating, eyes closed again, to one NYC poet. You initially wanting woman Pres [not that you love Hillary]. Poet, Boston postie's daughter, slim man's shirt, cigarette jeans. Nice boots,

Régis Bonvicino

fashionably slightly up at toes. Who, at very minute maybe flying back *into New York / and the season / changed / a giant burr / something hot was moving. . . .where's the fear / I asked the / Sun. The birds / are out there / in their scattered / cheep. The people / in New York / like a tiny chain. . . . .*

Eileen Myles

Today, happy. [Nervous]. Walking to meet younger poet. Still in sweltering city. Who standing, dreads softly tied. Absorbed in Blackberry. Outside South Asian resto. You 2, circling round each other [delicious vegetarian curry]. In way of strangers at lunch. Loving he coming from St Louis. A little like chez nous [you divining]. Bearing some old-fashioned French-inflected style. Elegance. Plus leadweight particular Catholic stamp. Of continent's horrific colonial crimes. And misdemeanours. Poet speaking, brilliant, eloquent. Re: your *My Paris* novel. Goth in its writing/acting-out of being there. Immediate. You, stunned by perspicacity of his comments. Unable, though *Annotations* one of fave books ever. To be offering single brilliant commentary. In return. Digressing to tall tales [+ likely true]. Re: part-Indigenous Grandpa, Grandma, cousins, in-laws. Finally, at pause in self-conscious identitary prattle. Exiting restaurant door. You shutting up enough for poet to insert perfect question: How, in writing, were the Montréal *Théorie, un dimanche* group rinsing sentimentalism out of queer? Standing by great Italian sausage shop—named Murray's. You, devastated to have squandered occasion for beautiful literary discussion. Weakly declaring: "I

Keene

Louky
Bersianik,
Nicole
Brossard,
Louise Cotnoir,
Louise Dupré,
Gail Scott

have to go in + buy sausage for a Frenchman" [R's boyfriend]. . . .
LORD, will you ever stop?

Such as it began in the Jewish Hospital of St. Louis, on Fathers'
Day, you not some babbling prophet but another Negro child,
whose parents' random choices of signs would disorient you for
years. It was a summer of Malcolms and Seans, as Blacks were
transforming the small nation of Watts into a graveyard of
smoldering metal. A crueler darkening, as against the assured
arrival of dusk. Selma-to-Montgomery.

Keene

A vapid damp. Rising from flagstones. Laid over SoHo former
wetland cobbles. Threatening to ruin gleaming page-boys of 2
elegant strolling women. And render limp cute netted **40**s-style
hat of rapidly trotting SoHo shopper. Were there to be a
downpour. Water rising instantly over cobbles. Covering former
bog. THERE COULD BE A FLOOD! Humidity + elevated
temperature. Forecast to be raising humidex to "Dangerous." As
you

Arm'n arm with R. In from The Green. Entering Werner Herzog
film. Re: melting Antarctica. Slow to point of mélo. In dark Film
Forum, she getting up + wandering. Bulgarian women's choir
—very 'in' this year—singing, haunting, in background. Then to
excellent SoHo French bistro. Lightly salted Euro-style fries.
Maghreb-grilled chicken. You commenting finding Jewish friends
inspiring. "Cause ever keeping on the run." R, embarrassed: "To

23

get away from those running after." Her friend, dressed marginal, watching. Disdainful. From other side of table. Later. By way of smoothing over—sending 'politically-aware' e-mail. Coming out smug-Canadian: *Hi R. Still trying to figure out how to write in this place. So focussed + quick. Do lack of social nets determine urban gait? Surprised to have enjoyed Herzog film. Usually feeling about his work like you feeling re: background Bulgarian choir, heavy, sentimental, moralizing.* Avoiding mention of creepy huge dead cockroach. On floor. Hard + gold. Extraordinary long feelers. Her cats eat 'em up. Sign off: *Rain nice, chills me a little . . .*

Slinky as 7-of-swords tarot card thief. You sneaking [*toujours* 5:30a!]. Off SoHo box-pattern sheets. For purpose of parsing Dem primary polls. In hopes she. Whom media treating as old-bag-with-baggage. Polling less tireder-+-tireder. In press photos—laughing less. Mouth wide-open, cartoonesque. Almost. Compared to O. Witty. Cool. And on good side of generational divide. Had he not voted, 4 years in Senate, far left as anyone? Walking under his social-realist looking poster. Radiating promise.

[FURNITURE MUSIC's playing current Federal election campaign. Chez nous. Where incumbent right-of-centre Mr. SHHH's former pastor. Said leader of church against abortion. Divorce. And homosexuality, basest of sins. The Church—

somewhere near Calgary. Boasting coffee bar. Soft-rock band. Shopping-mall-sized parking lot. Three giant-screen moving images of elders serving communion. Magnificent foothills of Rocky Mountains in background. Mercifully Mr. SHHH promising. Not to reopen gay debate in Parliament.]

So WHY. When black poet arriving from somewhere on coast to visit. You pointing to a *Guardian* report. Mocking Obama-boosting liberal US media. Taking itself—reporter sniding— ... *as more superior and detached than it actually is.... Let's hope the consequences of electing "the one" will be as wondrous as the press has led the voters to believe.* Your visiting poet, author of precise, yes, Harold Evans beautiful, work. Composed in high-treed, many-windowed flat. Somewhere East of city. Where, evenings, also running small publishing venture. Excellent avant-music [you imagining]. Playing in background. Now shaking head sadly: "You, Gail, don't understand a thing."

.... Since noon, there has been a group of whites marching along the edge of the park, cheering for the grass to be cut. They worry that we are doing drugs in the weeds—that the colored people are. Because I'm lying in the grass, representing that scenario, the noise is loudest around me. They chant *Save our park!* and *We can't see the trees!* in unison. These are people I imagine filling the offices of downtown.................. Renee Gladman

SO, IS THERE NO BETTER OFFER THAN OUR EVER RECONDITIONED SUBJECTIVITY?

Édouard Glissant

One might also ask. How—in trying to penetrate OPACITY of difference—to be avoiding bias? Fostered by sentencing's compulsive lean-back. On precedent [A *single grin with lips pasted*

Lisa Robertson

back]? Which precedent oft setting track toward over-simplifying outcome. In rapidity of binary altercation. To point of rendering intersectional complexities invisible. While at analog end of spectrum. Such complexities deferred. On behalf of Citizens, too tired. To be absorbing anything. But the trivial or sensational. On TV evening news. *TERRORIST ELF ON 42ND! HIGH COST OF HOLIDAY COCAINE! PONZI SCHEMES ON WALL STREET!* To hypnotic tune of background newsloop printers. Printing recession bank-rescue dollars. [Because they (the Treasury) can!] Even rich a little nervy: . . . *last night we stopped the car . . . & I watched people on the verge of ruin. How many Rolls Royces, & other low, pink, yellow, very powerful cars weren't booming through the park like giant dorbeetles, with luxurious owners, men & women, lying back, on their*

Virginia Woolf

ways to some party. . . .& we on the verge of a precipice. Whereas

Your precipice at moment. Mere chronic claustro. In slow studio down elevator. Momentarily diverted by blonde Euro-French woman. Telling boy-child over. And over. *Combien elle adore les bananes.* Her tongue flickering in + out. Rounded pink lips dying to suck or bite. Those Euro-French! Ever overplaying naughtiness. To other great republic! It's your mocking meme. From *la belle province de Québec*. Bobbing into stream of Citizens. Hurrying down vehicle-choked Houston. Past ghosted Twin Tower hole in sky to South. Past Broadway. The Bowery. Narrow park. Likewise framed in fuming spitting gridlock. Ere disappearing behind retro SUNSHINE CINEMA glass façade. For *Man on Wire*'s daring dizzying [**08.74**] skywalk. Between near-completed towers. The funambule having crept unnoticed. Daily, for weeks. 107 floors up. To be laying 200 feet of wire between Capital's highest markers.

Ah, those risqué French again! Funambule Philippe Petit's light slippers in cyanic haze of Manhattan dusk. Groping out on high high strand, near-invisible from ground. Wind aggressed minuscule pointed feet swaying across/back, 8 times. Cops on other side, meaning Petit abruptly sitting. On wild swaying wire. Somehow back up on feet in vertigo-producing leap, a little spot in sky pirouetting on tiny gust-whipped thread. Which hero. When cops release. Fucks beautiful young girl in New York loft. Who wanting to be first to welcome him back to ground. Says his French girlfriend: *After the Towers, our histoire came to an end*. His ex-best friend. Likewise standing by him for months of daring undercover schlepping of wire-launching equipment past construction crews to top. Deported. Weeping as he tells of end of friendship. You wondering, exiting cinema. If cruelty hallmark of so-called genius.

Now. Old Re-pub McCain. Waddling across screen. With dishy Alaskan VP pick, Sarah Palin. Clasping pretty Down Syndrome baby. Several other handsome children. Following behind. [FURNITURE MUSIC playing ruffed grouse + babies crossing road in the country.] Eldest teenage daughter. Said impregnated by hockey-star boyfriend. Someone dubbing: *Sex on skates*. And whole North childhood passing before you. No living room with antlers. But Alaskan Palin's favourite dish, moose stew [she's right about moose!]. Oh no! Now she promising to be drilling. In most pristine wilderness left on planet. Chanting *Drill Baby Drill*. In unison with Re-pub audience. Veterans in hats. Veterans in tears. Odd dark face in striking whiteness of context. R saying just like Althusser—Republicans knowing it's about ideology. "They can put tits on the ticket."

Excitedly, your Campers. Flat soles for lean-back posture. Again hotfooting East, past Houston/Broadway fruit stand. Semi-basement bars. *Recent* 'ANTIQUES.' Onto Bowery. In cool effluence of 'people like us.' Entering low scrubby black-painted Bowery Poetry Club architectural relic. Mid bourgeoning glass-+-gray condo surround. Crowd profiling as in **40**s film chiaroscuro: New-York sculpted. Or rangy. Flagging poetry's role in the culture. Making of *random function*..... an *organizing agent—visible, tactile, part of our sense of the world*. On tiny front-café bench, girl, mouth open. Nodding on hunched shoulder of writing guy beside. Pushing through saggy corduroy curtain into dark

Joan Retallack

club bar. You noting one shaved head of a Frenchman. One blond US dude, stomach protruding—"Oh! *You* here now?" Poets' cushy asses on folding metal chairs. Whose work some calling unfeasible, inasmuch as being *variously fragmented, occulted, difficult, and silent . . .*, work *that critics who champion the work have gone to great didactic and theoretical lengths . . . to compensate for the loss of traditional aesthetics. . . .*　　　　　　　　　　　　　Oren Izenberg

On dark stage. Single bulb over. Poet, fedora at angle. Shouting ALL WRITING INVOLVED WITH TRANSLATION. No　Bernstein final text being sacred thing. [Conjuring 'translation' chez nous. Where any sidewalk stroll soliciting slip/slide from one tongue to other. Implying utterance perpetually re-interpretable.] Fedora poet holding up thick volume. Its Huichol yarn-painting cover image of bright animal/human/sacred threading. Editor of reissued *Technicians of the Sacred*. Being *also* anthropologist/　Jerome private collector. Here offering amazing *range of poetries from*　Rothenberg *Africa, America, Asia, Europe, and Oceania.* Poetries crucial. To intoxicating **1960**s radical reset of culture values. Their mind-bending "formal things like parallelism, + weird juxtapositions + amazing musicality, all implying powerful critique of Western rationality." Fedora poet now reading eerily prophetic refrain from Athabaskan language: *Water went they say . . . mountains were not, they say . . . Fish were not they say. . . . Deer were washed away they say . . . Herons were not they say . . . Then otters were not they say. . . . Then snow was not, they say . . .* Magnificent　Athabaskan
Poet
[unknown]

poem of decreation. Lyric. Yet *not* single speaking voice of Western lyric ego. "SARAH PALIN AND THEOCRATIC FAMILIES WERE NOT THEY SAY." Calling out Fedora poet. Inserting critique of rightist Re-pub VP candidate Palin. Deemed provincial to point of hysterical. Into the '*It was very dark.*' Of Kato poem. [FURNITURE MUSIC playing Palin's high-pitched voice as if an auntie's. (Also loving moose.) And you want to weep. For your mother + her sisters. Alberta Bible Belt with whiff of outsider rebellion.] Your feet, crossed in browny Campers. Listening to magnificent poem after poem. From oft dead or dying Indigenous languages. Happy these radical no-longer-young poets having youthfully engaged with same. One after other. Coming up + reading, prancing, growling. Performing sense of some measure of familiar. With these long-ghosted others. A woman's standing on her head. Innocent as **1968**.

Stock market tumbling. Tumbling. Re-pub hopeful McCain. Saying economy fundamentally sound. Dems instantly heaping reams of ridicule. News videos streaming newly jobless. Today, well-put-together slender hard-working finance professionals. Leaving Lehman Brothers Investment Bank. Carrying belongings. Conjuring unemployed of Great Depression. *SAVE, now, media covering* those walking singly. Carrying pricy suit jackets. Smoking slender cigarettes. End-of-term Bush. Looking rapidly to left. To right. Like cowboy. Mantra of let-us-continue-to-be-Americans. Resilient, hard-working. Albeit lacking whole hog optimism Citizens admiring. In foundational Whitman's fresh new American sense of time. *I celebrate myself . . . / And what I assume you shall assume . . . What is commonest, cheapest, . . . easiest, is Me / Me going in for my chances. . . .* You, in your North way. Walt Whitman Pausing at *and what I assume you shall assume. . . .* What hubris! To speak with supreme confidence. For the many.

In Wooster windows opposite. Wide-screen OBAMA. Calling, in soaring folksy yet erudite language. To rust-belt workers. He later said to have abandoned. . . . *by . . . rejecting unions, subsidizing Wall Street and big business and embracing deregulation and privatization.* Language so brilliant, so beautiful. Some saying winning Robert Reich Presidency with poetry. Who himself self-defining as ". . . *blank screen on which people of vastly different political stripes project their own views*." Perfect. If electoral system requiring its leaders to be Obama gathering requisite widest middle into 'Citizen.' But O. In representing middle. Needing to beat retreat. From Chicago hometown parish pastor/mentor. Which reverend having declared, post 9/11: *We bombed Hiroshima, we bombed Nagasaki, and we nuked far more than the thousands in New York and the Pentagon and we never batted an eye . . . and now we are indignant because the stuff we have done overseas is now brought right back to our own front yards. America's chickens are coming home to roost.* O saying problem Jeremiah Wright being [white?] people. Not getting that black pastors often priding themselves on speaking with clear *prophetic voice*. Re: social + racial injustices. Not wanting to pressure parishioners

—adding *Times* commentator—to agree with every word. But,

rather, to spark thought. Representing: . . . *a cultural, a stylistic gap.*

[FURNITURE MUSIC silent. No ideology chez nous. Able to be drawing Francophone, Indigenous, historic anger, toward centralizing cohesion. PLUS. No foundational revolutionary war emblemizing exceptionalist notion of Citizen. However fictional. North party politics being dispersed + regional. Indeed one may be voting, decade after decade. For ever-losing 3rd party Social Democrat option. So what? Who cares? *Sorreee* . . .]

Having hidden. Weeks. From blazing streets. Sliding, on this Depression-type day. Off meager patch of sun. On box pattern sheets. In search of tiny autumn rays. Mid shadow-casting high buildings. Trying scorching dusty bus-stop bench. Moving on to stone wall of NYU's Silver Towers quadrant. Trying to read Stein. On governance + identity. Under stone-cold eye of huge flirty Picasso *Sylvette* sculpture. *If there was no identity no one could be governed, but everybody is governed by everybody and that is why they*

Stein

make no master-pieces. Moving again for sun. To business school square. Suits milling chaotically. Notwithstanding bank bailouts. To calm the disaster. Late-afternoon vagabonds. Relaxing on benches. One stretched out on left side. Facing bench back. Pees. Piss's meandering down slight incline of square. Till running between legs of your chair.

Walking home down Wooster. Past century-old Caffe Dante. Little iron-legged tables. Other men. Neither suited. Nor destitute. Enjoying conversation. Tiramisu. Prosciutto. Espresso. Classic back courtyard. Layered air-conditioners. Fire escapes. As in film noir sets. Then passing, in recess of building. Newly homeless guy. Very clean. Donning huge earphones. Settling down on cardboard. Long-tailed shadow deking low into black garbage bags. Just ahead. Opening steel studio door. Those ugly black plastic rodent poison stations you hating. At both ends of radiators. Upgrading in mind to notch of reassuring. In bathroom, alas. Giant red cockroach. On back of toilet. [No point keeping toothbrush.] Likely headed to kitchen. Closing bedroom door, tight. Waking, morning. It on dresser. Staring intensely. Like a pet.

Real events, occurring in real time, . . . [that are] *transformed in the act of writing them. . . . toward a 'new time'* . . . [notwithstanding] *illusion that . . . 'the adamant social being / is inner'* . . . Perfect for Leslie Scalapino 'hybrid' individual in your identitary/non-identitary *Obituary* novel. Ever on line between appearing [exterior] + disappearing [interior]. Then losing her in computer!!! Hours trying to recover. At 4p, walking to financial district. To check ambience mid economic chaos. Buildings rising like masts on narrow curved streets. With lovely names. *Pearl, Maiden, Water.* . . . Winding down to port. Stock Market's huge Stars + Stripes stretched across the 6 iconic frontal Corinthian columns. Once upon a time in **1970**s. You, proto-Bolshevik, entering. With artist from Stockholm. Watching from upper gallery. Deafening brouhaha of marketeers screaming, yelling, selling, at each other. On stock market floor below. "*Chaos*," laughing Swede, "*in the heart of capital*." Back to dirt cheap loft he renting in SoHo. Big freight elevator opening on space. Rather cold + damp. Ni fika på kaffe och fikabröd.

Today. Liquid powder blue. Dizzy playing background. Gail happy. Dems predicting landslide. Below window. Male noirish-type Caucasian. Performing low-level super-empire exceptionalism. Suit frippy at edges. Fat stomach. Squirting open mouth with breath freshener. Rare still green trees bent over cobbles, grey-gold under brick + yellow-hued buildings, narrowing toward huge blockwide Telephone Co. building. Filling vista. Eiffel-like telephone towers blinking on top. The telephone. Ringing twice in village where partly growing up. Signaling to all secret party-line eavesdroppers. And stout not young but beautifully groomed telephone operator Dorothée Marcotte. Whispered to have a lover. As everybody knowing. Cause in tangled networks of human conglomerations ... *the telephone is the unseen link between a million lives. . . . . confidante*

Lucille Fletcher *of inmost secrets. . . . . life and happiness wait upon its ring. . . . .*

T to dinner. Having just published *Unexplained Presence*. Exquisite treatise re: black women in mainstream cinema. Dampening former liking for French director Ozon's *8 Femmes*. [That scene of gorgeous no longer ingénue Catherine Deneuve. And Fanny Ardent. Rolling on floor.] Which Fanny also liking to visit black maid, Firmine. Who *lives behind the big house, in the hunter's cottage, where at night she entertains the Red Rose* [Fanny], *a "fallen" woman who plies her wares on the wrong side of the tracks. In her hunter's cottage, Firmine is madame, silky, sprawled across her duvet in a black negligee, a cigarillo between her lips, mooning at her love. Red Rose sits on the edge of the bed, laughing from deep in her throat. They play cards; one trumps the other. Firmine's eyelids grow heavy with waiting for the moment when this innocent game will end, and another, more satisfying one will begin.* T arriving. Carrying pretty glass vase. We drink, we eat, we talk. Round midnight, descend to street to smoke. Leaning against wall. Watching SoHo go by. Ere she stepping into night.

Empty glass vase. Sitting on the table.

Tisa Bryant

2008 *bis*

MUSIQUE D'AMBIANCE

Having failed to cancel Montréal tickets for Gertrude Stein conference [paper appalling]. Staring out rue St-Denis second-level 'Tourist-Room' window. At shiny suits rushing along New Orleans-type verandah. Floor sloped for snow runoff in winter. Down outside stairs to street. Some skinny derelicts, staggering or clomping. Dirty beige rags. Beckett-gray wind blowing dry autumn leaves. Students in low-cost polyester nicely put together. Low buildings' brightly painted trim. Bars. Bars. Bars. Gail, drinking espresso + reading *Le Devoir*. In café next closed storefront where once upon a time comrades editing revolutionary newspaper. Till day next-door bar owner finding, on redoing common wall, your 'headquarters.' Wired for surveillance. Later same Sunday, pistol in upper B&B window opposite shooting passer below. *Règlement de comptes*, people saying. Your wide pants, fitted brown-+-black houndstooth jacket ['leopardskin' lining], likewise recalling old kitschy lawless Montréal quartier-latin days. Now disappearing behind old stone church façade. Hiding French-language university. Leather folder under arm with shaky conference paper. Probably overstating how writing in English in Francophone Québec. Impacting [as per

Gertrude Stein in Paris] sentencing. For one, French syntax/ cadence enhancing lingual gesturality. In local English. Given French sentencing's tendency to be axed on the verb. While English sentencing classically more descriptive. More oriented toward object end of phrasing. Knowing on very thin ice. Now invoking Stein attempts to attach language to body. Ergo to gestural of physiognomy in speaking. Blushing to roots at essentialism of proposition—further suggesting visitors to city observe expressivity of Franco lips in profile. While with many Anglos speaking. Lips scarcely moving. This, grad students loving. But great Oulipian, having offered conference splendid mathematical grid for reading of Gertrude Stein in Paris. Looking scornfully [single long hair coming out of chin]. At Gail requesting he sign book. And US critic, resplendent in saddle shoes. Declaring local GS's sentences. Nothing like Gertrude Stein's. Plane. Taxi to SoHo. In rain.

THE POETRY SEASON

Now coming perfect fall days. Warm [a little smelly]. And—*poet knocking at door*! Sculpted shoulders in second-hand magenta silk shirt. Making mockery [you thinking]. Strolling along Prince. Of SoHo fashionistas. Who, having learned, junior year in Paris, to tie a scarf. Sashaying along beside. Expensive bundles scrunched about their necks. You 2 in flickering blue-y breeze. And fading leaves. Floating out ahead. Toward **70**s rock diva's place. Or was B, in saying "place," meaning not diva hangout café? But semi-detached red-brick residence. Opposite café window? White posts on either side of door. Recalling hitching-posts. In front of Grandpa's Alberta jewelry store. Not to mention diva's album *HORSES*. Brilliant overdrive anthem to molecular proud abusive everyday. IS NOT HORSE THE EPITOME OF THIS? You loving how B across table coded. Like any Northern. By childhood's hypnotic empty snowscape. Beyond grid of Indiana door. Plus deep scar on upper lip. Making beauty fierce.

Walking through coals into a city within the fire
entering the ember, encased in a protective suit
to bring out handfuls of what that world inside of burning wood is like.   Brenda Coultas

Stocks sagging more. McCain. Finished. Liberal press also relentlessly ridiculing prospective VP Palin. Who replying to journalist's query. Re: preferred reading material: "I've read most of them [newspapers/magazines], again with a great appreciation for the media." Asked to name specific publications. Palin responding: "All of them. Any of them that have been in front of me over all these years." Obama, in reply to same journalist question. Citing Toni Morrison's *Song of Solomon*. Plus Shakespeare tragedies. Plus . . . *The Bible.* . . . Perfect!

Friend sending from Paris: Poster reissued from May **68** uprising. On half-century anniversary. Calling for

G.RÊVE GÉNÉRALE!

The period in *G.rève* [strike] underscoring that dream [*rève*]. Integral to **60**s massive worker/student revolt. Causing Gail, in tizzy of nostalgia. For when art experiment/class struggle indistinguishable. To be scurrying East. Fast as any SoHo-sidewalk budding neo-liberal. Not wanting to board Greyhound bus. Back home. Up Bowery. Over Churchyard. Already at podium: North Language Poet. Speaking compressed near-claustro lines. Aimed at pulverising any notion of speaker self-expression. [Some Lesbians smoking outside, *not wasting their time.*] But you knowing poet rarest of Anglo-Canadian. Supporting, during North country's near-secession battle with Québec: Great Franco-Québecois *automatiste* Claude Gauvreau. Whose *Jappements à la lune* [Barkings at the Moon]. In lines

Steve
McCaffery

like. . . . . *ghédérassann omniomnemm wâkkulé orodècmon zdhal irchpt laugouzou* . . . Marking—Anglo declaring. Admirable disjunction Claude Gauvreau *between meaning and the phoneme.* Sitting there, on St Mark's Parish McCaffery Hall folding chair. Sinking deeper into warm bath of nostalgia. You reminiscing [**1973**] Montréal performance. Of suicided Gauvreau's sound-torqued play, *Le Charge de l'orignal épermoyable* [*The Charge of the Expormidable Moose*]. Performance opening senses to point that, on exiting théâtre. Gently falling snowflakes. Pounding on head. Another of tonight's poets. Beautiful, tiny. Behind podium. Huge scarf around neck. Declaring that whether any line pointing to meaning [or not]. Essentially question of time:

> *"Time" she said, declining his epidemic.*
>
> As if serrated, Welish

On bench. By Hudson. Sign saying: *Natives called this estuary Mahicantuck.* No mention of . . . dare you say—GENOCIDE of same? Mayor, at downtown 9/11 Memorial, himself daring to cite Sioux. As if personally owning words exiting his mouth: *We are related to all things and animals and people. . . .* How that computing in his resource-sucking city? On dusty fallen-Tower site. Row of photos, weathered, obliterated first-respondent faces. Climbing climbing stairs in collapsing buildings. Sad men are throwing roses on little pond. Near under-reconstruction Tower replacement. Said to be progressing moderato. Slow, past end of creaky Hudson ferry quay. Chugging huge liner. THE NORWEGIAN SPIRIT. Brawny water.

Iceland government
Bankrupt completely.

Crossing St Mark's churchyard [some graves, some rats]. Poetry Project director S's mentally decrypting other graves. Across those brawny waters . . . *at the western end of Long Island Sound. . . . a 101-acre Potter's field, . . . largest tax-funded cemetery in the world. More than 850,000 bodies are buried there. . . . inmates from Rikers Island are tasked with conducting the burials. . . .* Entering Parish Hall. Packed with people breathing mousy dust of that loving nest. The poetry community. Enjoying sitting, together, against world of platitudes + mediocrity. In wake, decade after decade. Of great dead or elder Master poets. Big men. Ginsberg, Auden, O'Hara, Berrigan. At podium. Slim woman in jeans. Slim high-heeled beige ankle boots. You seriously craving. Poem on birthing. Your lezzie mind having drifted to life's other . . . *limit*: S's cemetery. Reached Styx-like by Staten Island ferry. Where

one million exhausted bodies touch
totally compos mentis ex-missile flue
empathy of cold terror air
conduits brainwaves where the wardens
prohibited themselves.

Mysteriously. To write *Master* piece. One must be refusing identitary parameters. In order to be avoiding self-censor. In mirror-face of others. But how to write if no imaginary addressee,

Stacy Szymaszek

Szymaszek

Stein

you wondering? Heading toward street provisorily closed to traffic. For Citizen play + intersection. Which street turning out to be bereft of people. So over to exponentially swarming bumper-to-bumper Broadway. Woman on ATM sill. Rolling sock. To scratch bites. Couple ahead—heading to Chinese Olympics. Four of those new smartphones between them. Every time ringing. Mutual convo deferred. But *NOT* [inner Bolshevik grousing]. *In old Dada spirit of deferral as nonsense-procedural contra capitalism's forward-appearing profit-logic acumen.* Right onto Prince. Jam-packed with sidewalk vendors. Desperately hawking bags jewelry scarves. Faux designer logos. Shoulders rounded, eyes darting left, right. Being, you projecting. Of menaced migrant situation. None performing high-flying alacrity of earlier-times Bowery Street pedlars. Selling garbage-picked goods decade or 2 back. *But human nature is what the city grows best. There are peddlers laying out books in rows on sidewalk or tabletop, very good ones, and shoes lined up by size and color. One peddler ran after us saying "I will not be undersold." The merchandise pulled out of garbage, reasonably clean, ready to wear, and ready-to-read very good books.* Conjuring Beckett's derelicts, for whom: *For each one who begins to weep somewhere else another stops. The same is true of the laugh.* In boutique window. Polka dot scarf of avant filmmaker friend. Her films—*Mayhem, Covert Action, Cake + Steak, On the Downlow, Fucking Different New York*, etc. Abounding with polka-dot women. The better to express ebullient femme-resistence?

Coultas

Samuel Beckett

Abigail Child

Palin ever more relentlessly parodied. By media. Now [jokingly] said giving birth to 6th. While being interviewed on [Tonight] show. To Northern, her pink lip diction ["How's that hopey-changey stuff workin' out for ya?"] Kind of Daisy-Mae mimetic. But is not US body politic oft vaudevillian? Joe the Plumber. Aka Joe Six-Pack. Palin's prototypical working man. T-shirt fitting close, shaved head. [And Ruger handgun on table when interviewed some years later.] At other end of spectrum: That sexy ultra-short-shorts bus-pole dancing woman. Performing hot crush on Obama. Highjinx *unthinkable*. In Canada. O, himself, in pre-election ad. Seated, performing. In Oval Office facsimile. As if already President. Complete with faux-Presidential crest.... Giving new meaning *to all notions of political advertising.... part slickly produced reality program; part Lifetime biography; and part wonkish policy lecture with music that could have come from "The West Wing"....* Performance, reporter adding, *acutely Middle American: suburban lawns, American flags, corn fields and factories ...* You, shocked. But Québécoise friend Mad laughing with pleasure. At 'theatrics.'

Jim Rutenberg

Which perceived US Genius. For high-culture/vernacular fusion. You, today attaching. To Saturday afternoon BPC poet. Desultorily performing faux-[white?] desperation. *"The way all knowledge is guilty." "Modesty as tool for mayhem." "A bitter pill."* Later to be adding to list of apologia: *"Fisting myself with the American flag until I see opportunity."* Lines in disjunct or

Michael
Gottlieb

non-sequitur relation. Landing between high-brow desuetude + faux-transparent flat language. So one continually turning head. In order to be grasping sub-rosa message. DIRECT-*SEEMING*—but actually quite INDIRECT. Conjuring noir-like stock-phrasing. *I want to report a murder / ... San Francisco last night / Who was murdered / I was.* Accompanied by close-up of suspect or victim looking DIRECTLY into camera. Eyes bright + glowing. Like gaze of huge-eyed cockroach in studio. Soon also to be eliminated. Later

From *D.O.A.* (1949)

Same night. Standing drinks. In Bowery loft of left-wing poet/ editor. Stained pressed-tin ceilings [precisely as chez nous]. Front room kind of old-time factory ambience. ROOF press books tucked layers deep on shelves. Trees in front of windows. Antediluvian computers. The ROOF Publisher. Being employed somewhere on Wall St. Explaining to polka-dot filmmaker. How housing bubble evolving, mortgage + credit being *products*. Bought + sliced up each time for profit. Till on paper worth, say, 35 × original. Increasing, increasing sub-prime mortgage rates. And folks unable to pay. Causing bubble to be bursting. Completely. "Fascism!!"—Language Poet exclaiming. Then to Cajun resto. Reasonably priced + Cajun 'heat.' Improving on much modest-priced local fare. [Two salads—one tuna, one chicken, pasta, steak.] Male poets at one end of table. Talking to each other. Women at other. Mostly queer. You hearing Lang-Po say again: "Bank bailouts = corporate government fascism." You like him.

Has he not offered e-mail of partner. Very cool dancer? Herself also dealing with giant roaches? A lot of people not liking Language Writers. At all.

DEPRESSION MONOPOLY

Stocks still falling. Out Café Pécan window [Tribeca]. Citational 1930s Paris: Corner streets fanning, 3 directions. Subway entrance on diagonal. Art Nouveau glass-+-iron. Also. Excellent long espresso. People sitting at laptops. Gorgeous woman entering. Dark straight hair. Late flapper-era cut. Almost see-through leopard-pattern top. YUM! Voice saying: "Everybody playing Depression Monopoly."

Guy jumps little fence. Looking for something in hedge by bank. Scrambling frantically, obsessively. In brambles. Woman, older. Gray. Gray hair. On chin. Sitting in fenced community garden. Where last night dead rat. Student, anxious, reading sales brochure. In smelly supermarket. Man asking for 'credit'—they do that here? Young woman cashier so tired holding body up by leaning on counter. You projecting 3 part-time jobs + long commute to children in outer borough. Because

Class always reigns. This, being prime connection with E. Sitting, front row, Polish Hall. Pointy skinheads on screen. Yelling *Bring*

back Auschwitz. At gays marching in Krakow pride. *Two* Brazilian
men leaning over. To tell Gail how nice, Canadians. [For
legitimizing gay marriage.] E + you then heading out to eat.
Question of inviting Polish lesbian spokesperson to join. Who
maybe dying to breathe some queer American air. But nice
[possessive] Canadian opining that likely changing
conversation.... Then at table for 2, sneezing sneezing. From
cheap red wine. [And guilt re: Polish woman.] Walking home
—dude trying to sell E a rose. They telling him he getting *all wrong*.
He handing rose anyway. Yelling *BULL THAT DAHK*. After
awhile E saying IRS seizing bank account. To pay, they joking.
For bank Krasch bailout. You admiring how they knowing to 'roll
with the punches.'

Raising window a crack. Analogous Krasch-apt aphorisms rising
from sidewalk. "Nail-biter." "Up for grabs." "Watch your back."
"Pie in the Sky." Advertisement-like jargon. At which—bragging
conservative *Times* commentator—USians bettering Chinese.
Who ... *see business deals in transactional, not in relationship terms ...
People who create great brands are usually fulfilling some longing of their
own, some dream of living on a higher plane or with a cooler circle of
friends ... Many of the greatest brand makers are in semi-revolt against
commerce itself....* E.g., Stewart Brand, the hippie creator of
*Whole Earth Catalogue ... That compendium of countercultural
advice appeared to tilt against corporate America* [sic!] *... embraced by
Steve Jobs ... and many other high-tech pioneers.*   David Brooks

Our Northern. Leaving familiar [boring] SoHo. Climbing late. Past marble gaze of Center for Fiction paters. Who founding, **1820**. Locale for shielding innocent clerks. From vices of immoral city. Via fostering *correct taste in reading. . . . . . . the voice of wisdom has made itself heard, and many who were wont to devour pages of romance alone have become readers of history and lovers of science. . . .* centuries later. Friend K. Singing wildly delightful poem. On creamwhite, dark-wood trimmed centre stage. Arm tattoo hidden. By sleeve of little Michelle-like dress. You eyeing at dinner. In her apartment. Whose bedroom window framing Empire State Building lights. Red. White. Blue. Sometimes yellow. Next reader of evening: LA lawyer + Conceptualist V. Skin very pale. Jet hair. Suitably suited in citational Dada. Reading from giant brick. Calling up, collage-like. Multitude of cadences. From giant dispersed Southern California home

Vanessa Place

city. . . . Featuring ... *voices of television shows, screenplays, and medical books juxtaposed with the intimate narratives of a rebellious young girl, a doctor performing infant cranial surgery, a corpse accounting for his own death, and a truck driver on the road with his*

Stefanie Sobelle

wife. Then E. Reading in laud of weirdness. From *The Importance of Being Iceland. . . . Since I was simply glad to have my name in the New York telephone book when I arrived, why wouldn't I want my name on the* [Presidential] *ballot. But to achieve that meant ONLY gathering signatures for 18 months, which would have erased the opportunity to give speeches. And speaking was the point. So I campaigned to be a name you wrote in. Some of the pay-off was that at ages 40 and 41 I was a*

youthful candidate. . . .Weirdness I've learned always pays off . . . Then <inline type="margin">Myles</inline>
T. Reading from her heartbreaking tales of erasure of black
women in cinema. *Imagine a world of false windows, frames filled
with still images. Unchanging windows. Imagine yourself. Picture
yourself. Seen from the point of view of the unseen. The unknown. The
unnamed . . .* <inline type="margin">Bryant</inline>

Yellow taxis to Lower East Side Pink Pony literary café. To be
closing [**2013**]. In continuing demise of old LES low-rent era.
Hearkening to when poets affording to be freer: *18th st. or canal
east on grand st. travels coming brighter over / haze suns toward little
italy rudolf bass reads / brighter than it is red green & violet sky coffee
shop coca cola / grand & broadway flooded with rain or turquoise light
/ green light red light out the back was smoke rising or cars / passing or
numbers letters lathes on scoops drill down.* We girls round back table. <inline type="margin">Bernadette Mayer</inline>
Horizontal to wall. Brick. Shelves + shelves of bottles. Books
shelved very high. Sometime on diagonal. As if commenting
contemporary art mode of displacement: *Pure Conceptualism*—to
be writing a Conceptualist [they were everywhere those days]
—*negates the need for reading in the traditional textual sense—one does
not need to "read" the work as much as think about the idea of the work.* <inline type="margin">Place/ Rob Fitterman</inline>

Gail + E ordering nice juicy burgers. The LA woman, 2 or 3
salads. Several espressos. No wonder so white. E commenting
high percentage of lezzies. Having borderline personalities. Gail
exclaiming: "My exes! Especially one, singularly unattractive
personality." Conceptualist reproachful. Unless that *tch-tch*
ironically approving your directness?

Tonight. Already near dark. Shortening days. Direction—>
upscale WHOLE FOODS. *Whole week's salary.* Sniding former
cashier. All-aplenty in autumn orange of pumpkins, yellow of
squash, red of apples, mums, roses lemons, giant cauliflower,
brown mushrooms. Young couple ahead. Girl with little white
lace-trimmed slip over jeans. Verrry in this year. He having been
hunting. A lot of liquor, it was kind of fun: "The first time I ever
killed anything + ate it, it made me feel alive."

[FURNITURE MUSIC's playing amie lesbienne in Québec. Just
North of Vermont. Speculating men ejaculate when making very
big kill. Lovely mountainous area crawling with poachers in
prodigious vehicles. Guided by village men, chronically
unemployed. Which 'guides' bragging exploits in local bar. While
undercover ranger egging on. Till half of village men. [Briefly] in
jail. Someone saying police patrolling. Knowing they poaching.
But afraid to stop in remote situations. Cause everybody armed.]
And if Mr. SHHH winning again in North. Long-gun registry to
be abolished. His base needing guns. Without which:

> *It will not work with the bear*
> *who, like the Indign, has to be shot to be*
> *made good. . . .*

Rachel Zolf

52

LEANING ON ST MARK'S POETRY PROJECT IMMUTABLE STONE WALL

Eyeing star-studded autumn sky above. Lost in glare of city lights. Gail pondering, as per. What impact poets living in singular small-group existence having. In relation to wide-empire thinking. Inversely. How train of preceding generations impacting present St Mark's poetics. Especially those foundational **60**s St Mark's bards. Who having turned from hyperbolic emotion-laden **50**s Beat-era resistance. Toward new *deflationary diction.* Thereby abandoning ... *overheated, hyperbolic, charged-up, emotion-laden styles associated with the prophetic, confessional, "beat," "projective," and political poetry.* ... *Deflationary diction* [providing] *a powerful counterforce—a negative dialectic—to fighting ... outrage with outrage, suffering with expressed anguish, self-righteousness with self-righteousness.* ... Swerving *away from the bombastic rhetorics ... apocalyptic thinking associated with ... the H-bomb, and of the strident anti- and pro-communism / capitalism of the Cold War.* Or one could say those snazzy post-Beat **60**s poets   Bernstein
abandoning 'authentic' melancholy. By getting out more in the sun: *It's my lunch hour, so I go / for a walk among the hum-colored / cabs. First, down the sidewalk / where laborers feed their dirty / glistening torsos sandwiches / and Coca-Cola* ... Among early Project   Frank O'Hara
poets: Formidable AW. Writing, late **60**s Spontaneous, direct style: *People come into the world to live / & go out when they're totally exhausted.* And, recalling time as Project director, when poets   Anne Waldman
were

Waldman

. . . .far ranging, their field was much more open, expansive.
So-called subject matter was sexually explicit, tender. The poems
were political, spiritual. Lines were shocking, dissonant, powerful,
beautiful, lyrical, strange. The audience stayed with these poets all
the way. Responsive to the point of shouting out commentary.

Contemporaneously. To be tracking Citizen Poet in post-millennial Manhattan. More like *Lesson in Art of Deferral.* Poet's feigned or real addiction to displacement. In current Krasch-deflation era. Reining ludic O'Hara stroll. Into time-pressed oppidan trot. *Appearing* direct + to point. Yet—at any given opportunity. Whirling out of pattern. As per [one could say] minuet in Louis XIV court. That *bourrée* [double-step] with polka-dot filmmaker X. Who—notwithstanding your pre-arranged brunch date. Sliding into tiny alcove with lover. Being, upon your arrival. Halfway through the Sunday special. Or that *half-coupée* [sink-+-rise] of Publisher. Forgetting rendez-vous to which you will have [**11.12**] rushed. Over hurricane-devastated streets. Bouncing up + hugging. Or *promenades* with R. Where you understanding 'forward' when she abruptly back, or to side, right foot, in very small steps, then left, then right again. Expressly pointing, 2 or 3 times.

The less you (I) leave the house the more autobiographical the work
becomes. I have given you something—was that my intention? A
confession? No sooner made than over: I have left the house. In fact,
Levitsky
I've gone to Florida.

That other, famous, American GS. In perceiving such US restlessness of verb. Via borrowed Euro-French lens. Declaring Americans liking to be on move. While speaking in very clipped phrases. Contrary to French. Who ... *feeling that they are and indicate and feel moving existing inside them ... Any American.... knows ... just how many seconds minutes or hours it is going to take to do a whole thing.*   Stein

Meanwhile, our Northern. Marking time. One whole hour on platform. Train after train. Speeding down middle track. She having failed to notice.... *Ambient and atmospheric interference has produced (and by atmospheric I do not mean the same thing as ambient, I mean ... carbon monoxide, ozone, loud noises warning emergency or arrest) a formidable barricade, against which our ability to focus on each other gets lost or is absorbed, even when we are physically near* ... Thus,   Levitsky
entering, in usual dream-fog, wrong station. Then right station, wrong direction. Then stuck at 50. Arriving 1½ hours late. For coveted date. R non-nonplussed. At dark stone court table of Flatbush resto. Reading, very focussed, xeroxed document. Eating pan-roasted chicken. Luscious, juicy. You ordering the fish. *Flasque*, mediocre. Next her gleaming bird. Talking imminent elections—you to be venturing [*again*]: Obama so-called socialist. R mildly: "In blood sport of two-party politics, correctness less desirable than capacious electability." Walking you to car service. Arm around shoulders. Loving her Canadian. Home, in studio, nice Canadians on TV news. Voting

substantively to right. Again! Meaning Mr. SHHH just short of majority. Puckered up, kissing blonde wife Laureen on lips. Tee-totaller thimble of champagne.

Maybe to say 'people like us' meaning all of those. Whom young poet EK naming—by proxy. As compunctious. . . . *i used / to sleep*

erica kaufman

on the floor. wed to / the want to reek of exclusivity. Referencing, you guessing. Not only 'i.' Of poem. But also students, profs, any of we professionals. Who failing to feel responsible. For part in current disaster. Hence relieved [as any neo-liberal]. By Fed's decision . . . *to print dollars from thin air . . . creating $1.3 trillion that did not exist to replace some of the trillions wiped out by falling house prices and vengeful stock markets*—the Fed to have *taken troublesome assets off the hands of banks and simply credited them with having*

Peter S.
Goodman

reserves they previously lacked.

While the privilege screen mechanisms
continued on their language mission

disclosing to certain entitled persons
things withheld from the majority of humankind

Evelyn Reilly

(Wikipedia/apocalypse définition two)

THE PROVOCATION IS THIS . . .

A HELEN ADAM HALLOWE'EN: In window-barred coconut cream St Mark's Parish Hall. Lovely Southern-born NYC poet singing sweet homage to late Scots-born-American Goth bard, Helen Adam. Ex-Southerner having in common with late Scots daughter of Presbyterian minister. Poems appropriated from Church music. Music, oft rooted in folk culture/wisdom: *I learned from my Mom and Girl Scouts and church camp songs which were strangely vaudevillian . . .*, minor key music *originally folk love and drinking songs. For me, Tuli Kupferberg first manifested the model* of tune appropriation in *"I see the White House and I want to paint it black." Rebby Sharp did that too. "Hard Rain's a-Gonna Fall" became "Hard Acid Rain's a-Gonna Fall." Helen Adam turned "Black is the Color of My True Love's Hair" into "Black is the Color of My True Love's Skin," that terrifying ballad that deals with lynching.* Which song 2 poets [**10.08**] now performing for Poetry Project crowd. In scat response to Adam's version of same: The lynched black man calling, calling. As flames engulfing ankles. Name of white lover Laura. But Laura/Helen failing to hear [listen?].

Lee Ann Brown

Julie Patton/
Erica Hunt

HALLOWE'EN 2 [MAD LOVES FESTIVITIES]: Mad, la Québécoise, writing in French in Manhattan. [Hard thing to do.] Stepping from elevator to avenue. Two fur-trimmed lavender masks in hand. So that you 2 looking continental. Standing 3-deep on sidewalk. As Hallowe'en dancing horde frugging up 6th.

Bathed in strange brown light, like old Brueghel [the younger] paintings. Proof, declaring exhausted florid-faced female parade director. Of energetic spirit. Of resilient-in-worst-of-times New Yorkers. Which New Yorkers, scoffing 2 Downtown bards. All crossing bridge from Jersey. Or somewhere. In frantic scant-clothed mass, 15/20 abreast shaking butts. Little ruffed skirts. Bare breasted. Tattooed. Papier mâché masks. Black 'Obama' kissing white 'McCain.' Prancing voting booths. Conjuring shower stall in *Psycho*. Huge skeleton ghosts leaning half-breadth of avenue. Great drum band from Harlem. Feathers. Drag queen majorettes. On + on they come. Racing uptown at crazy pace. With Krasch looming quiet like background set in theatre. TV news downright Shakespearean: Actor playing Mafioso in iconic *Sopranos* TV series. Arrested. For real-time armed robbery. And Tea Party Obama-haters protesting somewhere. In tea-bag fringed hat-rims. Or high-crowned basket-weave flag-decked inverted flower pots. Utterly foreign to Northern.

Having [oh dear was that 1 of those strong sleeping pills I took, or 2?] stood between rows of triple-shelved second-hand books. Eyes averted from R's delicious décolleté. Whose lips close to ear. Whispering [... you forget]. Having descended late. To panel. On *Race + Poetry: Integrating the Experimental*. Then having been fretting. Seated in last row of basement seats. Book-weighted shelves above. Maybe causing ceiling to crash down on heads.

Plus wanting panel to be more revealing. Re: black avant practices. Till panelist counselling mostly white audience to worry less about blackness. And *more about whiteness as purchase.* YOU LIKE THAT! Was not that your vaguely passing family? You're a liar.

The provocation is this: that among African-American artists who engage in experimental and avant-garde practices, there is a distinction that often leads to a kind of "identity trouble." ... *The trouble is that black artists are concerned with the experimental, the edgy uses of elements that some may judge to be out of place within the precincts of such ("avant-garde") practices: the hint of the image within an abstract pictorial field, the use of voice within an otherwise language-based poetics ... such a worrying leads to an unnecessary narrowing of what constitutes avant-garde practice....*

Geoffrey
Jacques

11.08: ELECTION DAY. Having been meaning to read Plato's *Republic. The better* to be grasping how Citizen of Republic. Differing in notion. From subject of ex-Dominion. But something always coming up: The sun! Meaning, lounging on bed. On which it shining one whole hour. Through open bedroom window. Later, walking out. Today. Further East than usual. Streets, empty, breathless. Citizens busy voting. Preparing post-election parties. For he whom evening news reiterating. Running first campaign. Exploiting 'face-to-face intimacy' of social media. Not to mention speaking in tongue so poetic, indeed, almost Biblical. Having gained huge advantage over Re-pub McCain. Of late acting like not minding. If losing. Being old warrior just doing his duty. White guy ahead. Staggering on sidewalk. Open collar, shirt. You can feel his anger. Wide berth into very old flat. Door opening on minuscule kitchen. Small living room. Floor, sanded. Two lezzies, one joyfully inebriated. Single straight girl. And 2 poet couples. One of whose child named after *Moby-Dick* protagonist. Sound asleep on little cot. On screen, results rolling in. And small boys in Obama masks break-dancing. Unrestrained glee!! Tearful Howard prof, head down. Choking up. When mike thrust in face for comment on win. Auditorium of black students. Screaming in ecstasy. Yesterday, Obama to interviewer's question re: stakes of campaign ... "people telling me their stories: 'My wife has ovarian cancer, but she's out there campaigning for you.' 'My son for the first time has decided to apply himself to school ...' 'Obviously there is a historic dimension when a 90-year-old African-American woman just grabs my hand and will not let go.'" Gail leaving before champagne. Harlem place to be. But couple leaving with—changing mind. And going home. Gail, ruefully—>SoHo. Past bars full of celebrating up-+-coming East-side mostly white liberals. Cocktails of every colour. Past cool lonely dude in recess of Wooster building. Whose temporary cardboard turning into permanent dwelling. Late into night below window. NYU students wailing name Obama. Strange half-celebratory half-desperate chorus. On all large TV screens in windows opposite: Presidential victory speech. Michelle by his side. Stunning in flame-red + black. It taking 20 seconds for *ressentiment* to emerge. Michelle's 'dress from hell.' Her 'Black Widow' attire. Her 'lava lamp with a volcanic nod to husband's Hawaii.' Complaints about her cardigan. Yet had she bared her arms? Surely lewd sneering at beauty of her pecs.

What does a victorious or defeated black woman's body in a historically white space look like? Serena and her big sister Venus Williams brought to mind Zora Neale Hurston's "I feel most colored when I am thrown against a sharp white background."   Rankine

Against a *straight* white background [in back of head]. You scoping Catherine Opie's exhilaratingly queer, fleshily baroque portraits. At Guggenheim. With E. Opie's naked tattooed dyke. Pendulous breasts. Naked suckling boy toddler. Long legs curled comfortably, under other bare breast. Quelle madonne! Quelle ... cool appropriation of pious mother. Same pushing-toward-*l'extraordinaire*. Marking Opie's classic studio-posed portraits. Trans people. Drag queens. Leather dykes. Photographed with solemnity. Dignity. Almost regal. That unforgettable gorgeous full-blown white rose pinned to blooming crotch. Physiognomies' beauty in their ambiguity. Racial. Sexual. Heading back downtown. Happy! Free! After breathing Opie's boundaryless air. Then embarrassing attack of claustrophobia. In packed downtown sardine-can #6 train. Press of knapsacks. Bellies aggressively spooning—maybe pick-pocketing??? Waving, embarrassed, to E. Jumping off at stop. Small wait but delicious solitude in single seat. Near-empty southbound bus. The

misanthrope hated other people. But you in many public situations. Merely finding

re-entry meaningless and imaginary
falsetto

compositions

Welish

only when she was appealed to

To wit: East Village party. Where Gail hanging back under cordial arrow. On turquoise corridor wall. Pointing to cozy coat heap. In bedroom. Being incapable of approaching poet. Whose

Mayer

inimitable *Midwinter Day*. Topping, since summer. Bedside-table pile. Not to mention shifting gaze. When eyes a minute meeting woman's. In felt fedora. *Very* sad eyes. Being she who someone saying losing son to race bias. In LA hospital ER. *if i see death first*

Akilah Oliver

i'll tell him to treat you good. Another woman, hair piled impossibly high. Joking sleeping with O. Back when he at Columbia: "I met him on the train. Trouble walking after." At first you thinking she overplaying to gallery. Then thinking in sending up O. Likely parabolically mocking all these laughing whites. Who always enjoying stereotyping joke.

Thomas King

. . . the first rule of racism. Think it, but do not speak it out loud.

Alarm clock in other room. Punctiliously unplugged. Punctiliously still ringing. Ringing. Middle of night. Melding with garbage-truck beep. And state-of-emergency heartbeat. Re: upcoming reading of *novel*. To St Mark's poets. Falling back asleep, dreaming *job ad in newspaper. At new uptown hotel. Joining hundreds in line, all origins, beautifully attired, for handful of positions. More + more homeless. Taking refuge in ATM space in bank. Your stuff strung out on ledge. Scratching bite under pulled-down sock.* Thus, bleary-eyed, tardy. To uptown West Side lunch. With downtown poet guru. Mosaic tile apartment lobby. Nice earthy colours. Oak panels. Multiplied in mirrors. Little court garden. Two nannies pushing gape-mouthed screaming babies. As tightly bonneted. As Duchess baby in *Alice*. Poet's small, worn, book-lined living room. Paintings by terrific Susan Bee. Woman driving car, revolver out window. Guy passenger beside, familiar Fedora. The poet. Like nearly everyone you knowing. Obama supporter. Agreeing policies likely to be middle/conciliatory. Such as 'yes' to Afghanistan. To be keeping military happy. Cause pulling from Iraq. Sushi resto. Likewise dark panelling. Peace-enhancing glass waterfall installation. Chefs behind bar composing sashimi. So capacious. So raw + fresh, simple. You, sated. Feeling confident enough to be blurting that even if not poet. Offering, in your narratives, sentence relations. Close to poetic enjambment. Refraining from saying "hybrid."

[FURNITURE MUSIC's playing Vancouver poet's bi-racial father, proprietor of small-town Chinese restaurant somewhere in Saskatchewan. *When he hears himself say sloup for soup he stops suddenly and looks out at the expected embarrassed and patronizing smiles from the crowd. Then he does what he has learned to do so well in such instances, he turns it into a joke, a kind of self put-down that he knows these white guys like to hear: he bluffs that Chinamen call soup sloup because, as you all know, the Chinese make their cafe soup from the slop water they wash their underwear and socks in.*]

Fred Wah

Fedora poet civilly preferring term "sequence." To narrative. To keep meaning flexible. His narrative work mostly restricted to essays. One you especially liking. Re: mingled-mangled language. Streets *of shifting rhythms against modulating repetitions and the shapeliness of ... sound-sense; while, hearing Langston Hughes, one immediately picks up not only on the specific blues echoes in the work but how he modulated shifts into and out of these rhythms.* Poet's phone

Bernstein

ringing. Brief utterances to someone in Vienna. Pleasant. Something perhaps sad under. Belting trench. Kindly having enjoyed lunch. He turning home. Not before excellent subway directions: "If you want the local, it's against the wall."

Today. To CUNY prose talk with grad students. A nervy, vacuous white cloud. Floating over head. Over billboard for job-hunting women: *FACELIFT: IT'S WORTH EVERY PENNY*. Arcane hats in milliner window. Pancakes, crushed, twisted, flowered. Right out of *Alice*. Woman milliner, herself. Wearing half collapsed triangle on head. Perfect for talk on weirding prose arc. As means of expressing current issues. Of social demand. Certain poets in audience offended. By contention experimental prose allowing best of both genres. You retorting [mite defensive?]. It very possible to be importing essential aspects of poetry [vertical language/fractalled subject, prosody]. Into forward bent of sentencing. RG late in from Boston. Elegant locs atop head. Sitting straightbacked on floor. Asking Gail how to be rendering reader-coherent. Dispersed writing subject. You, tongue-tied a minute. By enormity of query. Gay respondent remarking—+ this perhaps in answer. Gail having written: *People finding me nicer in French*. Crowd, mostly girls. Gathering after. RG's arm around waist. Several blocks to delicious, spicy, Korean food. Walking home from 34th with E. Feeling airy a minute. Cannot this last forever? This quixotic art-council underwritten moment? Alas

Douglas A. Martin

Already first wintery NYC day. Beige sky. White-painted brick. Great jazz on radio. Day floating. Perfection. From writing few lines to. . . . already nightfall. Only few weeks left. Ha! If staying, needing job. Starbucks employment ad on table: Smiling young men in white shirts + aprons. Mothers raising for better. Similarly. At solo supper in Le Gamin. Young woman. Simply dressed, black cotton, mules, shiny long hair, makeup, attractive. Incessantly calling friends on cell. Couple finally showing up. After a moment—waiting woman to declare: "I'm not getting what I want. I work hard. I make the right moves. But I'm not getting what I want . . ." "Still, it helps if you're white," saying black woman. Of fresh-arrived couple.

E saying taught America classless society. *As an American I come from a largely classless nation. That's the official word on who we are as a people. Citizens of the luckiest country on the planet, the freest—land of opportunity.* However, landing in Iceland during very down post-Krasch moment. E loving not only *crazy gray and lime-green landscape, geysers, one of the oldest parliaments in the world. . . .* But also the *lesbian prime minister (Jóhanna Sigurðardóttir)* . . . + *economic comeback produced by supporting the people, not banks, and by investing more money in culture and social programs rather than making cutbacks.* On studio TV, ad proposing colon cleanser. To help pass comforting fried chicken, hamburgers, fries. Plus—halting weight-gain + bloating. Picture of colon. Caked as rusty pipe. Going out for glass of wine to calm nerves. Every resto closed save good old Le Gamin. So, again. Warming odour of yes—salted fries, buttery herbed [grilled] chicken. Now 2 older women beside. One, gorgeous curves, black lace. From Brooklyn. "You Jewish," asking her companion. "Of course," laughing the other. Sitting there, you thinking identity, like food. A comfort. Ordering the chicken.

Myles

Wishing to be Icelandic

Night flashes of fever, sinuses. So not flying home. To memorial service for greatest North feminist literary critics. Then 2 indefatigable visiting Québécoises. Luring out to Chagall drawings at Jewish Museum. One in early 20th Berlin courtyard

Barbara
Godard

theater. People in layers. Like those unfolding cardboard cut-out dioramas. On birthday cards. Or seasonal toy displays in department store windows. Happy. Intense. Dramatic [+ *pas à peu près*, saying Québécoise]. You loving lack of distinction between audience + spectator. How everyone breaking into chorus. That form of collective art. Said prefiguring US musical theatre. Then to Chinese Cultural Revolution show. Posters also vaguely dioramic in fashion. But in obverse relation to previous. Asserting layers of top-down propaganda. Occasional didactic slogan. In foreground. Displaying life in fields, all rosy-cheeked. And songs. And joyousness in work. Fourieresque to a fault. Back in studio. We drink to.... We don't care what. [FURNITURE MUSIC in background playing darkening *sforzando* accompaniment. To Mr. SHHH's proroguing of Parliament. For purpose of derailing vote. To bring down his minority. HOUSE OF COMMONS: CLOSED.]

Tonight. Happenstance-ly. On late, putative part-Indigenous Mother's birthday. Reading novel dedicated to her. For St Mark's-in-the-Bowery poets. Having exited cab too soon. Ruined hair walking blocks in the rain. Audience faces blank for opening few pages. Then suddenly feeling you connecting. *In Settler-Nun totally dark Room, the abruptly non-static ambience resonant with pummelling tamtamming of ice pellets hitting front blades of ploughs.... hurtling up rues Clarke. The Esplanade. Hotel-of-the-City. Coloniale. Henry-J. Drolet, Settler-Nun, etc..... Causing silhouette in dark end of Room to oscillate a little ... on railway-flat bed ... projecting, in lying legs akimbo, un-nice image. Simultaneously self-admonishing: La sécurité, c'est quoi? C'est … suspicious, avaricious! Meanness. Of self-imposed seclusion. Who wanting to be 'secure'? No free spirit ever dreaming of 'security.' Or. If. She. Did. Laughing! Laughing! Letting others almost in range, then slamming middle gallery door. Causing postie, raising rain-brimmed hat + handing mail through barely ajar crack, to lovely lips, with toothpick visible in corner, to be declaring:*

Scott *—You're a bitter little lady.*

E saying your ego should be ballooning. Other 'likes': One Conceptualist. One ex-student. Friend T. One Language Writer [devastatingly saying, years later. *Never* reading prose]. One future publisher. Two usually critical Canadians [oh my!]. Four fab Poetry Project women [SS, EK, CC, CF]. Naughty R getting directly to sex point: "Gail, you're so dirty."

Companion reader, left-wing Chicagoan. Writing admirably economic. Emblematic. *Sans* ever sacrificing intensity of utterance. You, avidly re-calling. Youthful desire to be writing over top of complexities. Yet maintaining them as *audible* in language on page:

> *of rain.*
> *Someone is riding a bus, too tired*
> *for everything   except what is right;*
> *a god has his back against the wall*
> *of a church in Birmingham;*

Ed Roberson *the marchers take to the streets.*

Proof what mattering in writing: Precision of selection. Something to do with *jetztzeit*—that sudden connection between deep unconscious. And external happening moment.

To wit: Spring Street Starbucks. Rain. Packed, noisy, people [radio]. Gail [unlike Adorno] loving all that jazz. Baristas shouting: *chai with cream, doppio decaf, mocha latte, iced ginger green.* Patrons standing, sitting, anywhere, balancing coffee on knee. Older SoHo couple. His shiny hatch. Her elastic jeans, glitter down side. Tucked in high boots. Guy, hoodie, rolled up pants, red kerchief. Wending through with box of day old goods. Lucky people with tables for computers. Outside grey. Greying red white brown buildings, different heights. Almost hiding sky. Rain stops a sec. Mild, though near Christmas. People coatless. Little green video screen flashing aphorisms on wall: GOD KNOWS YOU GOTTA GIVE TO GET.

Days progressing *direct*—>departure. At same *time. Time* feeling stopped. As in stagnant flat grey clouds. Over water towers atop buildings. Thermometer also stuck. Well above freezing. You. In some kind of trance. Processing return North. Meandering, into coconut-cream Parish Hall. For seminal **70s** *Midwinter Day* 30th anniversary group reading. In homage to BM's cold crisp *bright December*. [The kind you liking.] Which 120-page beauty. Said penned in 24 hours. *From dreams I made sentences, then what I've seen today, / Then past the past of afternoons of stories like memory / To seeing*

Mayer

as a plain introduction to modes of love and reason . . . all I can remember / Of Midwinter Day the twenty-second of December. 12 poets on stage. Each giving different poetic performance. Of elder poet. For . . .

Marcel Proust

In reality, every reader is, while he is reading, the reader of his own self. "I" being—in best writing. Simultaneously intimate + collective. BM, in cataloguing. What going into any *one-day* routine. Calling up everyone's familiar: Food shopping. Library. Cooking for children. Visiting friends. SEX. Whole reading ambiance. Like Sunday mass as child. Congregants standing. Sitting. Or entering. Exiting. Through creaky Parish Hall door. For smoke, drinks. Whatever. A lover. Directly in front. Getting horny, stroking companion entire time of reading. What fun they having after. The 'Girlfriend.' In flimsy short print cotton skirt. Over thick grey knit tights. Draped nubby fuchsia scarf. Over cotton top. Covering flat or non-existent breasts. He, Tom Cruise-looking. In some kind of pricey long-sleeved tight-fitting jersey. Breasts last, saying R. Tonight all in brown. Little brown pumps stepping along beside partner. *Yeah*, thinking envious [minimally endowed] Northern. *With strong straps + wire.* Who having meant to stay one hour. Staying all 3. Following BM's lines on page. Flushing to left/to right. Space somehow enhancing SEX-charged winter ambience. Or it's just you. Waxing nostalgic for precisely that sex. On precisely certain bygone [North] winter days . . .

> *Snow is white crystals*
> *Hall mirror,*

Sad. PARTING PARTY. Winter storm [slush]. Devastating death
in community. Floating over. Worst imaginable for any parent. T
arriving early. Smashing in black dress, brown ruffs. Huge pot
delicious Caribbean soup. E mannish in tie. Tweedy jacket.
Offering *Vice* mag girl-ass-in-flowered-cotton-undies on cover.
Plus "Iceland Melting" essay. Suggesting melting glacial island to
be becoming geological *theme park . . . for how the world could change.*
San Franciscan BG. Basket of pheasant eggs. East Village B [+   Myles
man]. Homemade dove cookies. The Conceptualists. Sitting
creating text for Gail on studio floor. Roses on table. Red
tumbling curls of Euro-French woman on sofa. Spilling out from
luxurious Russian fur hat [ex-KGB boyfriend]. R + partner from
upstate NY. Through stormy sleety solstice night. Somber quiet.
Grieving, like most, here. Absent poet, poet's daughter. Passing
in Venice. One Lang-po, bright red + black almost Harlequin
cowboy shirt. Somehow right for moment. Whispering *Keep it up.*
You bring people together. You asking what he making of President-
elect's cabinet. He replying: "Obama's a nationalist." You—
having voted yes on **1980** Québec independence referendum—
countering: "You know where nationalism can lead." He nods.
Irrelevant.

Today, Harlem! Exiting train, 125th. Snow falling. Sparse. Guy
selling Obama memorabilia. Buttons. T-shirts, etc. Taunting you,

passing: *No more White in the White House / Black Pres-i-dent / In the res-i-DENCE.* Next block. Two dudes chatting up pretty blonde at corner ATM. "Where're you from Dorothy?" ... "Idaho" ... "You're a long way from home." Little farther on. Guy in lavender fedora, fur jacket over lavender pants + shoes. By famed Apollo theatre. Head nodding, laughing at. Or with. Fundamentalist sermon. Issuing from upper window. Then to *Studio Museum. BIRTH OF THE COOL.* Portraits, confident stylish **60s/70s** youth. Postures formal, colour-saturated. Against monocolour backgrounds. "Lawdy Mama." Beautiful young woman, dark-clad. High Afro. In frame suggestive of medieval icon. And other portraiture styles. Culled from art history. Artist to be [**07.16**] remarking. He resentful black artists—but never white. Always asked how black affecting work. *Given the fucked-up-ness of American culture, we can say that everything (I've made) is political, but that's not the case. My painting "Lawdy Mama" (1969) is a good example. Critics and writers likened her to Kathleen Cleaver [activist and wife of Black Panther Party (BPP) member Eldridge Cleaver], but the woman who posed for that painting is my cousin. It had nothing to do with the Black Power movement. I get irritated by this. . . . . I made a series of works called Michael BPP. I knew him when he was a Panther, but also when he left—his attire completely changed. I made three paintings of him in total. That connection he had to the BPP did not color my whole representation of him.*

Barkley L.
Hendricks

Rushing in early dark. Mid tony SoHo Christmas shoppers. Ecologic paper shopping bags. Preferred in better 'hoods. Three-piece brass band. Tooting on corner. Old songs, Dickensian. Gail trying to be writing every moment, à la *Midwinter Day. . . . Strange day [up at 7]. Daughter, bf, rustling in semi-dark studio—plane earlier than mine. Best Christmas ever.* Simple *6″ tree on dining table. Roses—cheap from corner Mexican store. Hyper fresh chicken [instead of turkey]. From Italian butcher. West of 6th. Waiting in line, wet snow falling. Guy behind, really liking Canadians. Telling your daughter how lucky she having Canadian mother. An artist,* himself. *Married to Canadian. Former gallery in SoHo. Now too commercial. Repeating really liking Canadians. . . .* You guessing Canadian wife holding up. Pretty well.

Snowstorm. Wondrous airline offer to defer ticket. Thus avoiding New Years' party. To North. True, given melty brown whiteness of NYC landscape. Once changing ticket—missing 'up there's' better snow. Crisp + hard. Masses here on this coldest December 31. In years [mere −10C (14F)!!]. Crowding Times Square. Waiting up to 6 hours for icosahedral geodesic sphere to drop. Lit by 32,256 LED lamps. Twice as large as ball from year before. You, on way to R's party. Entering exquisite Spring St chocolate shop. Buying 4 beautiful truffles. Performing, for willing line of young couples. Older bravely smiling woman. Spoiling herself. On New Year's Eve. Subway dark + empty. R's small company tucking into

General Tao + discussing Judaism vis-à-vis Christianity. Christians are cruel, saying one. You shocked she saying this in front of Christian-raised individual. Who—however—in part agreeing. In background Israel bombing Gaza. Razing buildings. Killing 200. R, looking pained: "What are we going to do about Israel?"

Subway home, one greyfaced youngish drunk. One black woman in lovely fur-trimmed hood. Looking straight ahead. Two utterly nondescript middle-aged Caucasians. Guy reading tabloid bursting out. In incomprehensible [to you] language. From time to time.

2009/2010

FURNITURE MUSIC [MOLTO MODERATO]

Montréal, QC [**01.09**]: To be stuck North [*unfinished manuscript*]
is to be periodically demurring: ... *If the line simply continues
without being crossbred with the non-esthetic, nothing is ever created.*   Shklovsky
[Translation: *The bigger the megalopolis, the greater potential factory.*]

Still. Nice January day in Parliamentary Democracy. Snow. Not
too cold. Café table knife light over open writer moleskine. At all
other tables faces at monitors likewise wishing to be famous.
Nodding in glutted noonday sun. On radio stock barometer
reported to be rising. Meaning no more panic GREAT RECESSION
billboards. Up + down Broadway. Now that funky **1940s** "Snatch
and Grab It." Playing relaxed, happy, on speaker. Projecting worn
[**10.08**] runner. Rounding pocky SoHo sidewalk corner. Past
freezing AC'd café window. Calling ... *AUTHENTIC BLACK
ALLIGATOR BABYSKIN PURSE! RHINESTONE ACCENTS!!* Trailed by
little half-veiled hats of 3 SoHo boutique women. And gourmand
lips of Chester Himes lezzie, lean-back stroll, satin tailored
shorts, satin pageboy. And well-painted grandes dames. Clown
makeup in this place. Being preferable to looking 'old.' One might
also say

The greater the demesne, the more social-demand exacting estranging, yet spontaneous, artifice. Mr Warhol taught us that. Making of any visitor a poet. Who rounding, in her strangeness, a corner. Breaking *own identity by breaking syntactic expectation.* Which *en-jambe-ment* irresistibly drawing [her] *into bending over into the next line to lay hold of what it has thrown out of self.* With only barest hint of narrative. Whereas, in the familiar

Ineluctable. Sitting. Absorbing local Montréal moment. Till inner diegesis part of phonic tiling. Of brouhaha. Of neighbours. Of radio reporting at border-distance: First Black President. On slow train from Philly. Replaying for citizens amassed along tracks. Inauguration train of great predecessor Lincoln. Such intensity of faith, patience. Crowds. Standing for hours. Bands, laughter, a *strepitoso* celebration of Republic. Remarkable to Northern. People, also packed all the way back to Washington Monument. As Barack Obama's distinct cadence rising [Michelle superb, pale brocade coat, beside]. Over National Mall: *The road ahead will be long. Our climb will be steep . . . but we will get there.* Fedora poet to be calling Obama's "poetics" Emersonian. Inasmuch as . . . *always at that beginning; it is the promise of America.* Optimism seconded by Aretha [regal bowed hat]. In stunning ode to country. And by inauguration poet. Declaiming *today's sharp sparkle, this winter air, / any thing can be made, any sentence begun.* A Reverend getting in last word. Praying for . . . *that day when black will not be asked to get in back, when brown can stick around. . . .* All the while you

Giorgio
Agamben

Obama

Bernstein

Elizabeth
Alexander

Dr. Joseph
Lowery

Sitting. Day after day. As if stoned. [Benefit of winter.] Café lights twinkling on terrasse. Under snow filigree. Subdued repeat-timbre ambience that *doesn't upset customs; it isn't tiring; it's French; it won't wear out.* As is woman near front. Fitted black top. Loose black skirt. Drinking carafon of rouge. Every few minutes, getting up, putting on coat, hat, scarf, going out for smoke. Lot of dressing + undressing. Hardly touching food. One of those smooth compact bodies. Impeccable posture. Never focusing on hand-written notes. More than 2 seconds. As if Time. Sliding between fingers. Being in this town, cheaper. Than in hyper-energized land to South. Where new President instantaneously announcing he bailing out banks. For economic stimulus. And Left not missing beat. Loudly grousing Obama soft. On recession-guilty lenders. While Right plotting, with bitter application. To rid America of socialist. *Typical!* [inner Bolshie admonishing]: *Capitalist democracies cannot legislate progress, when fossil fuel, its plastics, especially its automobiles—economic fundament. . . .* Or one could say. To-day

Upon to-day. Seated. Near somatic. Over green tea. Weather sunny. Almost melting. Disastrous for legendary calming wintry-ness of place. Still, people speaking low. . . . . *melodious, softening the noises of the knives and forks, not dominating them, not imposing. . . . .* A music to . . . *fill up those heavy silences that sometimes fall between friends dining together. It would spare them the trouble of paying attention to their own banal remarks. (And at the same time it*

Alan M.
Gillmor

would neutralize the street noises which so indiscreetly enter into the play of conversation.) Now. Bored-to-death couple entering. Woman beautifully dressed—wools, tweeds. Slenderish brunette. Hubby, youthful fresh of cheek. Petulant curl of lip. She trying to talk him out of funk. Offering little empathetic laughs. He, near accusatory, bewailing problem at work. As if her fault. But having no trouble smiling at waitress. Grinding pepper on his shiny vegs. Woman not eating.

To-day. Waking, TEMP $-30C$ = EVERY TRUE WINTER DAY A VICTORY. Exiting 3rd-floor room. [Novel protagonist Rosine. Still dead/passed out on bed.] Snow-light blinding. When not filtered via gently falling flakes. Or [turning corner], harsh-blowing hard-packed granular. [We hardly getting *that* any more.] Needling the face. Just like esthetician Suze's dripping stilettos. In retro toe-galoshes. Needling dot-pattern in snow. To café door. Who yesterday, while needling your face to stimulate collagen. Recounting by way of analgesic. Tales of undercover cop Dad. Very violent man. Who in [**1965**] shootout with bank-robber ski-masked gang. Offing pre-teen boy. Feeling kind of bad—he going to parents. They saying glad you did. We believe he possessed. Still Papa [allegedly] depressed. On sick leave for months. At last being well enough. For fishing trip with fellow cops. On far-North lake. Bad wind blowing up. Boat overturning. "We never saw him again; never knowing if dead—or deep undercover." Sitting pink + smiling, very straight. Perfect streaked-blonde upsweep. Crisp white smock. Suze proffering hefty bill. Ere

Another solo—*je m'en crisse*—weekend. Mercifully, A, B, S, K, writing to say *missing*. So lolling in little café *bulle*, vague. Almost Proustian. Too bad red-head Anglo dude at bar. Descanting in awful ultra-loud French. On cell. The better to impress pale gf. Skinny white leather. Thin plum lips. Note to be playing *désormais*. Uniquely French radio. For accent. Save, now. On *Ici Rad.-Can.* —accent, in fact, *Inuit*. Recounting forced 1950s family removal to point farthest North. For Fed flag-planting reasons [the Russians were coming]. How cold that first winter in tent. Too windy to build igloos. No dogs, Mounties having shot to suppress nomadic life. Unable to hunt. Desperately hungry. Now *there's a plot!* How, in traversing eras. Colonial traces sinking deep, ever more suppressed. Thus, more indelible. This, after bad novel morning. Protagonist [inchoate origins] always disappearing. No point trying to glue narrative. Unless THAT'S YOUR PLOT! *Novus Interruptus!!!* Whole set dull as police chief's office wall.

Woman coming in. Élise you thinking. From high feminist era. Defining feature. Total pockmarked skin. Talking, talking in one's face. For love. Or mouth to side. Confidentially ordering 2 huge croissants. Hot chocolate. Adding sugar [not so much as you!]. Opening rad femme book [*La pensée straight*]. Then getting up + exiting. Without paying [so friend of waiter]. Into slanting

Monique

freezing rain. Where gulls flying sideways. Clacking. Prematurely excited spring coming. On news. Left now cackling Obama funding right-wing faith-based groups. President riposting he becoming Christian. On seeing in South Side Chicago. Religion's potential to spur social change. [Your mother, again.] But why this incessant rap? Re: presidential centrism? When everybody knowing Left/Right 2-step being price. Of mainstream politics. R to have written decade later: *I feel this* [post-**2016** right-swerve] *moment shows the mistake the Left and the queers made by turning away from liberation and toward pride and acceptance.* Encore

Untimely warm. Loud 3-clarinette/1-trombone weather. Gulls swooping in mellow light. Raucous. Horny. Crowding sky above in dark/light wrought-iron-fence pattern. Pleasure couple entering. Guy tall. Excellent brown-laced leather neo-liberal boots. Holding high expensive bottle of wine. Very happy looking at his bottle of wine. She short grey haircut, expensive subtly rimmed glasses. Could be Franco *or* Anglo. Likely professors [pre-digital humanities]. Their seminars consisting of grainy films from industrial struggles. Uploaded on large screen of seminar table. Ere leaving students to view film. While they retreating to office. To be enjoying quiet erotic moment. She having recently pried him. From a marriage.

Morning. Catapulting icy rain. Warming to seasonable April drip. I.e., *mouvement-ordinaire*. Such as Satie composing to play at civil

Wittig

Levitsky

ceremony or lunch. Yours, this day, being with local Montréal poet. Sex Pistols T-shirt. Tattoos. Ornate rings. And other silver jewelry. Who, having taken black powder to plump up muscles. Endlessly pushing back long towhead hair + getting up to pee. Joking in self-deprecating manner. He he-man. Repeating, ad nauseam, can't get it up. Also taking pills for that. Cruelly, you laugh. On account of ad saying if still erect after 4 hours. Go to emergency. Stepping out [small wine buzz]. Into breathy spring mud odour under slush. Following some sweet ultra-hormone-y undergrads up Mr. Olmsted's mountain. Good middle-class wool sweaters. Cigarettes. Winding easy, relaxed. Bursting with hope, politics, sex. Spirit of wanting change. Soon to be fomenting short-lived [2012] Montréal student revolution. Filling narrow streets with their beauty. Their rosy demeanour. And slogans for lower tuition + overall better social conditions. For everyone. Then conceding revolutionary principles. To sole gov promise. Of tuition freeze.

Day. Woke from dreaming in a car. Getting some kind of rad intel from rad-fem artist: *Some dispensation to perform!!* Still, you taking your time. Not forgetting, pre-performance. To be chatting up blue-collar types. Sitting round. Black T-shirts. Mullets. Tattoos. *She* [that rad femme] would never be chatting *them*. You are wearing short beige-crocheted or knit poncho. Ruff round bottom. Something indecent or fake about this. As if showing your ass. Laying on back. Holding one leg up in air. Feigning it broken. Sliding, leg badly bent backwards—ruffed-grouse-like—

along ground. In order to—by appearing wounded—be distracting any one. From hiding place of babies.

TROPISMS [SOME BARS/CAFÉS, SOME READINGS + THAT FRENCH WOMAN'S EAST VILLAGE FLAT WHO, IF YOU RECALLING. . . . . . .]

Easter [**04.09**]: Day always *implying* [for Mother] wild hope of eternal life. As per Resurrection Myth. What mattering being not THE FACTS. But vision of sublime miracle. Eclipsing toward misty edge of consciousness. To which edge we all in fact, eternally returning. Difference being, for sceptic or non-believer. Mystery lurking there, at edge. More or less indicible.

But. At last. Return to R's bright windy Brooklyn square. Named for popular [assassinated] president. Your face in upper window. Watching bent flowering trees. Blowing low over huge heap of bagged trash. ½ block up. Women in impeccable white calf-length dresses. Wide white hats. Entering low flat-roofed church. Gospel music issuing from open sash. Your eye of a stranger marvelling at how this town sucking—in its complexities. Your inner tired surrealist, proto-Marxist, idealist feminist, increasingly isolated older queer. And tossing, indifferent. Into face of Western lust. For Oedipal model of economic trauma [+ its constituent imperialisms]. Which theatre, you hoping. Soon to be seen as parodic.

Later, eating pasta/delicious tomato sauce. [Vaguely missing Easter lamb back home.] Eye now on table view of street. Dark as in a Jarmusch film. Lone vertical fluorescent red LIQUOR sign on corner. Night-swathed figures coming, going. In daylight, R saying, increasingly white. Meaning brick through window of new hipster café. She refusing to go into. More wars on radio. And on library shelf behind dining table. *Wars. Threesomes. Drafts. & Mothers*, from Mexico. Narrative fractalled, acoustic. Educed from past when characters ... *plasmatic, even invisible, ghostly, not solid; in fact, characters had no other architecture than that of mystical music.* Having earlier further subtracted from R's floor-to-ceiling library-to-die-for. Abundant with volumes from megalopolis's still vast bookstore riches. A *Zither* poetic. Proceeding in way of ancient stringed instrument. Thus *allow*(ing) *continual change of one's conceptions while reading.* Countless other volumes. Solemnly anointing this anarchist moment of serious disjunction. And in this room where R spawning visionary Belladonna feminist collaborative. You crucially falling upon copy of early 20th feminist [**1914**] manifesto. Extravagant, outrageous:

Heriberto Yépez

Scalapino

The feminist movement as at present instituted is INADEQUATE.

Women if you want to realize yourselves (for you are on the brink of a devastating psychological upheaval) all your pet illusions must be unmasked. The lies of centuries have got to be discarded. Are you prepared for the WRENCH?

There is no half-measure, no scratching on the surface of the rubbish heap of tradition. Nothing short of Absolute Demolition will bring about reform. So cease to place your confidence in economic legislation, vice-crusades and uniform education. You are glossing over REALITY.

Professional and commercial careers are opening up for you. Is that

Mina Loy   all you want?

Oliver   Or, as AO, one of best poets of generation, saying: ... *vaginas destabilize a voyeuristic master narrative.* Whom you first scoping in this room. Speaking low to adolescent son. Himself, straining to flee Mom's white-ish Belladonna literary salon. His eager young face rousing old gut-churning single-Mom anxiety. Albeit knowing you *not* knowing—when child black + cops preponderately white. With fâcheuse tendency to racial profiling. *A genocide*, AO writing, *that wears my face.* Four years later, at party. Your eyes meeting hers. Almond, tired. Under rim of hat.... [A]*ll around me ... moving time ...* : Oluchi gone, dead. Being poorly attended in LA hospital. All action within any given political system, political. To perpetuate that system.

Days later. Having repaired to that French woman's East Village flat [so Euro-artful domestic, pastel utensil handles, turquoise

80s-nostalgic metal table, impeccable white sofa, well-watered plants, needy cat, curls + that gorgeous Russian fur hat, all of which you craving]. Heading East, direction→Bowery Poetry Club. For AO reading. From *A Toast in the House of Friends*. For Oluchi McDonald [**1982–2003**]. Poem not only sounding unbidden silence of mother-grief in PUBLIC SQUARE. But daring, also. To be speaking that slippery ventriloquist Love's ecstatic desiring side. Of Mother love. Seated at front, Fedora poet. Himself grieving one likewise young. Talented. Raising plastic martini glass in homage. The reading so brilliant. Poignant. That in stepping out again. Street's hum-choke-cell-deranging traffic. Jarring self-absorbed 'mother' tempo. Which tempo ... *far from contradicting creativity.* ... *disperses fixations, and circulates passion between life and death, self and other, culture and nature, singularity and ethics, narcissism and self-denial.* Or one could say AO's genius precisely that of moving beyond *mother lover car cake run.* Somehow reconnoitering buried gamut *of "shared possibilities."* So that, notwithstanding terrible inner demolition. Continuing her trajectory. Pursuing doctoral studies in poetics; writing works ever reconnoitering *disfigurements in expected speech.*

Julia Kristeva

Oliver

Then, one February ... unseen for week. *(T)he writers Rachel Levitsky, Emily Beall, and I (Rachel Zolf) paid a locksmith $200 to break down the door to Akilah Oliver's Brooklyn apartment.... Coming upon her body, alone, in her bed.... The TV and the lights were on, (Judith) Butler's* Antigone's Claim *was open on the couch....*

Zolf

BUT COME HERE, IF EVER BEFORE,
WHEN YOU HEARD MY FAR-OFF CRY,

[**09.09**]: Today, walking up 5th. Dust, milky sun, gathering down avenue. Spattering over turnstiles into City of New York University. For *ADVANCING-FEMINIST-POETICS-+-ACTIVISM [ADFEMPO]* event. [B outside, hair flowing, sun on face in excellent photo angle. Going somewhere else.] Inside, women drifting from room to conference room. Panel to enticing panel. Like bees in garden. Unable to settle onto so many perfumed flowers. So much long-suppressed beauty. Panels on female subjects + subjectivities. Inadequately addressed in many contemporaneous literary spaces: *WHY YOU TALK LIKE THAT?*; or *IS GROUND AS TO FIGURE AS AMBIENCE IS TO BODY?*; or *EC(H)OPOETICS OF THE DISFIGURED LANDSCAPE*; or *INHABITING FORMS OF AN/OTHER*; or *SPEED YOUTH MOURNING*.

Walking about, you taking in ambience of explosive restlessness. Of energy bursting forth. After years of post second-wave anti-feminist backlash. Pushing back on what barely begun, **1970**s. Even now [**2009**]: *New York Review of Books* reviewing *306 books by men; 59 by women.* Liberal *New York Times* Book Review section: *524 books by men compared to 283 by women.* Ezra Pound writing [early 20th] that women's poetry not caring for *music or imagism.* . . . Women performing—Pound nonetheless conceding. *A dance of the intelligence among words and ideas and*

modification of ideas and characters.

Or, as inimitable JP putting in e-mail to R: *>Laid an egg in my head about side broads, egg girlfriends and howl. >An anti In Ass A moanyfisto? . . .> Can tell em anything. That the verizon is both vertical and horizontal, has omniscient omnipresent and oppressive powers ever broadening.> That plain ol bards lack the passion and shooting spirit of passiflora> so shd stay home and beat their beaks against the oven and rent >their clothes. Their children will become egg whites.*   Patton

Ever provocative E. In keynote. Musing on why needing to be insisting on word feminist—"Can't we just be?" Further, enraging Language School women—of whom several in audience—asking why not writing "about sex?" After which, E reading . . . *You made me smell. / I didn't smell at / all before I met you / smells are pouring out of / my clothes, feet, my / socks. . . . . stinking of love. . . .* If in   Myles
appearance, graphically 'personal,' E's work, you musing, too absorptive of border contexts + awareness to be mistaken for singular lyric voice:

There's a wolfish quality to a poet's character. You might bring one into your home ("It looked like a dog!"), but ultimately a wolf won't act like a dog, can't understand that she's in your home and (as wolf specialists tell us) doesn't distinguish between inside and out. Wolves challenge the safety of our world. So it's probably easier to keep one out of your house than to try to imagine what that missing thing looks like.   Myles

Bookending closing night of conference: Friend C of Detroit.   Carla Harryman
Language movement poet. Whose artfully estranging *A Sun + Five Decompositions*. Resonating as avant musical construction. In

movement triggered by light shining on Paris roofs. Conjoining with glancing reflector rays. Glinting off shipping containers. As far as eye can see, in Long Beach harbor, USA. 3 or 4 actors, voices, multiple. Entwining in call + response. Dérivant from perceived 'normal' patterns of conversation. So that language reverberating tonally. C in profile, voice affect, neutral. Male actor + poet RT, in cogent rejoinders [+ occupying space with forceful (plus damned alluring, it must be said) presence]. Whereas C's performance work calling for "full-body listening + response-improvisation." Feminism being . . . *about this possibility, of emergent expression and communication that is not decided in advance.* A gorgeously balletic criss-crossing among speakers. Intercut with sonic scraps of sax, guitar, percussion. Building/ releasing tension in proceeding. Later you following C + fellow performer RT down street. Toward Korean restaurant. Eavesdropping passionate discussion. On meaning of *collectively* occupying space upon the stage.

Rodrigo Toscano

Harryman

I (we are floating under it) *so the body is experienced as imaginary because we share a double experience.*

phase   *but the conversation is pleasurable because*

ends

                                        I don't know it

to continue   Northward
                                               north-

we are less concerned about the boundary between a body and a word

a study in slow time

to continue   I don't know

SUMMERTIME [**2010**]: ONE BREATHY
CITY WEEK AT *THE MILDRED*

Sitting. Leafy Tompkins Square Park. Having only last night been
sitting with women on leather sofa. In leafy Mile End. Montréal,
QC. Jesting how—by multiple outrageous means of vigorous
boosterism or uncouth or shocking performance. To make success
of our refusal to produce accommodating art. You asking: "Does
not being unaccommodating by definition = failure?"

R not yet appearing. In goldy light of prickly-heat dusk.
Glazing crowns of people coming, going. Kid, pale, very thin,
inner left arm taped in strips. Holding broom as if park employee.
Other thin arm searching deep inside trash receptacle. On stretch
of green, yoga teacher. Students on backs, too close, you thinking.
To reeking perfume of little fenced-in dog run. Exiting men's
washroom, woman. Neat short curls, short cut-off jeans. Walking
legs ajar as if from shit. Or pain. . . . But

Evening will come. R will at last be sitting down beside. In
heat, rats also coming out. One grazing R's sandalled toe. *The
ground beneath us cannot be trusted; we need new ground.* . . . She

Levitsky

remarking it feeling kind of funny. Crossing Ave A, one more. HUGE. Skimming past *your* sandalled toe. Trekking east, hot piss stench rising from pavement. Left on truncated street. School blocking end. Women on stoops. Warm Latin music, from open windows. Nobody doing summer like this. Now Northern turning into building called *The Mildred* [that high-voiced-aunt with *breasts like shelves*]. Greeted by fresh AC rush of air you formerly impugning. Cause little boxes in windows sucking out hot interior air. Into ever warming exterior? Now so comfy + cool. In flat. Now. New faux-wood floating floors. Cheaply renovated CLEAN bathroom. Even building corridors nicely kept. [Save bloody tampon on stairs.] Might not this whole parade of comforts. Be treated as *artifacts*. Of present? Avatars of betrayals. We finding impossible to retire.

Upper apartment window. Backing onto schoolyard of 60s-vintage building. Offering architectural contrast. To dominant silhouettes of early 20th Victorian edifices. School being perhaps site of redevelopment. City having *anticipated and actively planned this redevelopment since the start of the sixties*. Instituting *not only a violent reconfiguration of its own landscape but also a legal and moral revamping of its own discursive structures*. Each attempt at resistance to capitalism's greed [counter culture, feminism, queer civil + human rights]. Somehow overshadowed by class able to pay for lawyers. "Move to Detroit," punk Diva Patti Smith declaring. Low rents + squats being still available. For

Robert Glück

Samuel R. Delany

92

all manner upstarts + rebels. Like NYC back in cheaper decades. Opening apartment door. You thinking maybe this flat in same building writer SD describing. Way back then. This building called *The Mildred*:

The alley behind the schoolyard: beer cans flattened with the indent of an instep, one twisted (aluminum cans with concave bottoms were only a few months old) to a flaky rope, others just bent. D T K L M F, sprayed across the brick with an aerosol can of purple paint, lingered from when I'd lived on this block four years ago.

I said: "I used to live on this block four years ago."....

I glanced at the boarded windows, then followed her down the steps. "There used to be a doctor's office in here four years ago. Do we just knock...?"

In the vestibule was a side door. "Just go in, they said." She pushed at the door. "Their lights got turned off about a month ago or so back and no one's had the bread to get them turned on again." About a foot in, the door hit something soft: someone behind it grunted.

Delany

Leaving window. Sitting on hard deco-*ish* sofa. Before sleek deco-*ish* coffee table. At end of very clean apartment hall. Sexy butch beside. Warm. Flirtatious. Desire being even more requisite. When general struggle for freedom. For whatever reason. Taking back seat. So that ... *penalty-free motivation, and / the introduction of public toys / define happiness.* But if now time to be going beyond covenant of *hope*. And earnestly repeated *yes-we-cans*. Then to what kind of action? Next you 2 girls on sofa.

kaufman

Dominatrix cat. Daily commanding 5a breakfast. Ere producing largest turds ever to be scraped from litterbox. Companionably licking licking her little cat genitals. As girls snuggling closer. In this building. So suitably called *The Mildred*.

2011

LE BONHEUR

Vote early. Leave for Manhattan. May 1, eve of Canadian federal elections. Just as announcement Obama "getting" Osama bin Laden. Leading up Canadian TV evening news. Elbowing to second spot, "historic" Canadian vote. Thought to be ushering in unprecedented Social Democrat regime. Fellow Citizens, having got in chips + beer. For tomorrow's electoral joust. [Kind of like watching Stanley Cup playoffs, n'est-ce pas?] Treated primarily on their little screens. To crowd of joyous USians. Gathering in Times Square. For carnivalesque revenge celebrations.

"Only the worst tourists go to Times Square," snapping E. Tan pickup parked near Chelsea café. Where sitting with CR. In from San Francisco. To launch superb proem collection *Sherwood Forest*: *... I want to write Eileen* [writes CR] *but I'm feeling guilty, I'm too high. / I fold my muscles into wads and sleep soundlessly. / I can't remember my dreams, they crumble, a soft cake. / A picnic with Carla. She brings rosemary bread and astonishing pistachios. / She reads to me about utopias. / So touched and happy I float right up into the sky.*   Camille Roy

You, likewise in Manhattan. During first [2008] Obama election. When simultaneous Canadian elections seeming far away. And mite provincial. Compared to glorious first-term Obamas, heading toward White House. So riveted to US polls + news channels. Failing to cast North ballot. In absentia. This time, little-big country up there's exciting. Too bad Canadian mass media coverage of *North* hope. For Social-Dem change. Daily more despicable. Having, 2 days earlier. Already been second-fiddling "historic" Left vote. In favour of Royal Wedding. Family values being now top plank of every party. Were not nuptials of happy soon breeding couple. To be saving monarchy from itself? Who also, by extension. Glamorizing currently Krasch-distressed romance of hetero-normative family life. . . . . Maybe you just cranky. Hardly any of your friends. Living in kind of family implied by "family values." *Who's running this panopticon, anyway?*

Wake-up, 9th St/Ave A: No internet. Radio quiet re: North elections. They don't know, here. Don't care. But sun shining into J's upper-floor East Village flat. J-Museum you calling it. J being performance artist. Her flat stage set of objects. Sculptures. Props so beautiful, chimeric. Delicate red-orange tresses of 3-foot paper mobile. Curling gently. On breeze over still half-asleep head. Then sinking into vintage East Village tub. Warmed by ray of sun. Its stubby legs next small kitchen sink. Plywood board cover to lay over later. In guise of kitchen counter. Tender green maple leaves beckoning outside window. Paris in spring can't beat East Village. In spring. Light breeze, sun. Beyond 'grille' of balcony.

Conjuring old Beats, jazz. Kerouac. Or **60**s Delany + Hacker. On way to breakfast, blocks South. Turn-of-20th buildings. Red brick, pretty cornices. Dussied up to fetch soaring early 21st profits. [Meaning J soon to be evicted.] People strolling, village-like, almost. Now appearing round corner: S, director of nearby St Mark's Poetry Project,

> . . . . *out for water coming back with soothing spruce*
> *bath salts // losing the Power Ball despite Susan*
> *Miller's certainty of money from an unpredictable*
> *place // propping against iron fence gobbling spirulina*
> *// new rubber sheet for Cass stuffed in bag //*
> *expression of confidence followed by the ever so slight*
> *fear that patterns can't be broken // my therapist and*
> *gynecologist having basement offices // emerging into*
> *late summer dark Shulamith Firestone dead in her E.*
> *10th St. apartment all week*   Szymaszek

Opposite Tompkins Square Park. Half block down: Cafe Pick Me Up. Wifi: 3$. Plus decent double long. Some older locals, individual in raiment. Obese guy in wheelchair to cooing young French pair: American girls best avoiding mini-skirts. Knees too fat. Couple laughing, flattered. Some utterly miserable men. Exiting park gates. Soiled clothes hanging loosely over bony limbs. Proceeding shakily. Ah, but here's one. Jaunty as North Social-Dem leader Jack Layton. [Mustachioed, swinging cane, dubbed Jack-le-débonair by Québécois press.] Park guy leaning on wall for balance. Ere high-stepping gaily West. While North Jack on little screen. With motley bumper 100-+ crop of new Social-Dems. On way to Parliament. One, 19, summer job at golf course. One spending campaign vacationing in Vegas. Abruptly members of official Parliamentary opposition. While barely victorious rightish victor Mr. SHHH. Small tight smile + teetotaler thimble of champagne. Smirking at decimation of centrist Liberals. Will Left/Right polarization in House of Commons. Be mirroring US-style 'CULTURE WARS'? The *Times*, burying story. But getting essential: That Mr. SHHH, already having twice prorogued Parliament ... *from outset promising to make Canada DEFAULT-CONSERVATIVE.*

Is this beginning of CULTURE WARS chez nous?

Calling R in Brooklyn. To clarify what CULTURE WARS meaning in America. R, incredibly smart, perceptive. Whose lovely round behind you last night following up Bowery. Too crowded to walk double. Turning to announce. With usual irony. *She* foreseeing that O—even before downing bin Laden. At last on winning streak. Notwithstanding [as several commentators noting] endless Repub obstructionism. But *CULTURE WARS*, you insisting? She laughing—"It's we avant poets versus the academy." Checking, you finding predictably threadbare stock definition in Wikipedia. Digital surrogate for mahogany-cased *Encyclopaedia Britannica*. Mother buying from travelling

salesman: . . . *CULTURE WARS . . . in American usage is a metaphor used to claim that political conflict is based on sets of conflicting cultural values. The term frequently implies a conflict between those values considered traditional or conservative and those considered progressive or liberal.* Missing word? CLASS! People live in classes. Word 'class' herein bundled in mantle of exceptionalism. The better to conceal that . . . *the primary source of fuel is not emotion/identity but economic insecurity that turns into fury, paranoia, etc.* CR [red diaper baby] later addending: *Neoliberalism has crushed the lower half of the working class and this is treated like an act of nature. For example we give names to hurricanes but not layoffs. This erases the political choices leading to deindustrialization and job loss. The problem is that working class life in America has become increasingly hard to survive. No one can see this because neoliberalism obscures the reality of power and its impact on working class decline. We are given identity politics as a set of explanations but it is not sufficient.* While poet AW noting how . . .   Roy
politics of Empire chip away/as poetry attests. . . .

> *Spooky summer on the horizon I'm gazing at*
> *from my window into the streets*
> *That's where it's going to be where everyone is*
> *walking around, looking around out in the open*
> *suspecting each other's heart to open fire*
> *all over the streets*   Waldman

Likewise under North's still default liberal surface. Royals on our dollars. Signalling old colonial narrative. Still beating in heart of nation. [Here FURNITURE MUSIC striking up salon piece. For recent crème-de-la-crème Toronto Harbourfront literary festival dinner. Tone, diaphanous. With Royals hovering over table. Where Gail of Québec. Stiffly encased in her suit. Envying lanky British co-reader. Cool/collected in classy pair of jeans. The Brit at once bonding with Harbourfront curator. Over how Prince William aging. Segueing to whether Harry pure Royal *laine*. Harbourfront curator. Whose family—it turning out. Fleeing Montréal at height of Québécois Independence movement. Showing off pictures of embossed Royal dishtowels. Hanging in kitchen of his yacht. Parked somewhere out there. On Lake Ontario.

To packed auditorium. Gail reading work. Rich in department of sound. Voices coming in, somewhat rowdy. Novel being not only set in pleasure-loving Québec. But also featuring several party-loving ancestors. Who—though words of Karl Marx or Walter Benjamin or Gertrude Stein may issue, torqued, from their lips. Seeming in face of all this Royal talk. Un-classy. Then Brit performing. Rather than reading from book. Decent stand-up comedy. Appealing to Toronto crowd right away. By commiserating with audience that Prince William + bride. Skipping Toronto. On honeymoon trip to Canada. Line of women, some men. Snaking round entire Harbourfront auditorium with arms of books for him to sign. You grateful to nice elderly Jewish man. Originally from Montréal. Standing alone by your table. With copy of novel. OK, pretentious to say this reading indication of CULTURE WARS' dark clouds. Thickening to North. It's *your* CULTURE WAR. It's lonely here. Between the genres.]

Saturday, the Bowery. Poet JS. Californian. Tall, blonde. Great boots. Nervous. Diction kind of *Howl*. Updated. Poem cowritten with San Francisco left poet/editor DB. Rife with citizens, angry, tired dwellers of parking lots. And dirty, cluttered landscapes. Perfect epigraph: *We work too hard. / We're too tired / To fall in love. / Therefore we must / Overthrow the government.... We're too tired to overthrow the government....* JS having been teaching in Hawaii referencing 'occupying government.' Term *gouvernement occupant* also historically de rigueur. Back in high independence era chez nous. Alas, leading Francophone *Le Devoir* paper [on East 9th still expecting to hear French]. Today touting vast hydro project in *"notre"* vast north ... Um ... Aren't those *Indigenous* lands? Usual anger in pit of stomach. Plopping in heap of ashes. Bien sûr some accommodating gestures. To Cree people. In interest of cheap electricity 'we' all wanting. As consumers. Meaning 'we' all part of 'occupying government.' Poets crossing street to Asian restaurant. Green bowl over door. Where sharing amazing garlicky greens. Chicken. Tender pork dumplings. Steamed fish. So good. So happy. Till friend of JS's. Living in Albany. Thus getting North public-radio news. Asking: "What has happened to you Canadians?" You wanting to retort: "Mind your own *oignons*." But he's pointing to last great North river flowing into James Bay.

Juliana Spahr

David Buuck

Rod Smith

Soon to be *torqued by men to flow in opposite direction. Drowning caribou + poisoning every little poisson.* "How can you just turn around a river?" he asking. Twice.

Scott

Sweet May. Tender buds a-swelling. Boarding train at Astor. Direction—>MOMA. For experimental film panel. With polka-dot pal director. Waxing, riding train, romantic. Re: cultural treasures of grand megalopolises. Woman on platform, lovely voice. Crooning American pop songs. [Eyes on the ground.] Then "Besame Mucho." Conjuring fresco of exhausted physiognomies housecleaning. Or moonlighting, East Village evenings. Arranging flowers. Loading cans on shelves. How many jobs per day? Will such hard grind be increasingly de rigueur in North. With coming Tory social cutbacks? Which cutbacks? Only Mr. SHHH knowing for sure. Still, riding along. Feeling free, Baudelairean. In dandy new scarf. When guy boarding. Apologizing profusely. For being hungry. Requesting donations. Passenger noses glued intractably to Smartphones. . . . *If rape or arson, poison or the knife / Has wove no pleasing patterns in the stuff / Of this drab canvas we accept as life— / It is because we are not bold enough!* Would Baud have seen self, likewise. As bench-sitter of *detached privilege*—both identifying with + unable to escape objectivizing . . . Then MOMA security guard. Perfect male. Young, burnished, muscled. Absorbed, talking to friends. Refusing latecomer entry. Tone rising as Gail protesting panellist a friend. Chez nous, to have been insisting. Now, unknowing

Baudelaire

Bernstein

104

consequences. Shuffling back to train. Pathetically sniffing: "Thrown out. Like vagrant." Baudelaire's point . . . entirely.

Obama, shirtsleeves. *Encore* parsing terms of decision to "go get" bin Laden. Implying, now, it dice roll. Risking, if failure, huge embarrassment to nation. Implicit in his take on event. Idea that winners = those capable of risking. When opportunity presenting. *America can do whatever we set our mind to. That is the story of our history.* Yet in saying, looking drawn. Awkward. As if war mantel not good fit. *Times* writer, uncomfortable with Presidential gloating. Suggesting more diplomacy. While Re-pub in Freudian slip. Describing getting Osama as—"WE GOT *OBAMA*." You asking Haitian taxi driver if Obama trying too hard to be liked by Right. He delivering eloquent speech in French. On strategy. In politics. Honking way uptown.

Obama

Mornings in J's museum: Poetry in motion. Arcane lamp shadows, cat faces, riverboats for bases. Cutout face of Michelle pasted to sequined ginger figure. Books shelved, wordy spines to wall. Cause books—J saying—making lot of noise. Early, via bedroom window. Close to rear building. Guy 10 feet away coughing up stuff, showering. Child somewhere speaking Slavic language, fresh voice. Mother breaking into song. For visitor. This near-promiscuous proximity exotic. Whereas irritating, back home. Now rain. What better lullaby than early morning rain? Swishing through leaves outside window. Somebody's clock goes off, not stopping. A somebody likely already gone to work. Maybe one of black-clad silhouettes on sidewalk below. Rushing, tight pants, shoes, long tapered toes. Toward subway. Clock pinging annoyingly, rapidly. For hour. Otherwise day strangely quiet, good for writing.

Afternoons. Usual 9th St stroll. Slight smell of piss, warm sausage. Changing clouds—coastal ephemera. Spreading puffy ruffled flanks. To reveal come-hither blue. In ludique foreplay to ever closer stinky sizzling summer. Not the fleeting spring, chez nous. Rapid to a fault: Icy snow/rain. Four days later. Heat-wave. Always, for some reason, awaking adolescent high of dust. Exhaust. Hanging round idling boats of cars. Driven by boys, mickeys between their feet. Remembrance being *neither what happened nor what did not happen but, rather, their . . . becoming possible once again.*

Agamben

Glut of amazing poetry readings. Raising spirits. To point of evanescence. So that giggling way through $10 Japanese box lunch. With S. Your near manic talking. Talking. Recounting hilarious exchange with Customs officer. Looking startled in booth. Then bursting out laughing. At Northern saying visiting NYC. To check out downtown poetry scene.

> *what can poetry do it*
> *cant not not do nothing*

it must undulate w/ the 2:30 pm dance music the sole

patrons at stonewall.

Julian
Talamantez
Brolaski

Some old Stonewallers. Certainly in attendance. At Church Hall
portmanteau reading. Celebrating one of own: Tim Dlugos.
Downed by AIDS—at height of epidemic. The audience, mostly
men. Trimmed, gymned, groomed. Substantial grey hair.
Gathering in resistance of idea. That poetry ... *can be fragile and
ephemeral. Before you know, it's out of print, gone + forgotten. . . .* Some
lesbians. E in plaid shirt. Beautiful young girlfriend. And tiny
'pooch,' draped lengthwise on arm. Older men gathering round.
Eyeing E + alluring young lover. Envious [you thinking]. The
pooch's little brown mug. As E reading Dlugos poem. Hanging on
every word. With intensity of the besotted: *I'm in bed in the Plaza
Hotel, New York. The guy who picked me up is in the bathroom, and I'm
wondering what he'll want me to do, worrying that there's some secret
way of lovemaking between men that I've never heard of . . .* You, for
3rd time in single week. Delighted to point of euphoria. But

Harryette
Mullen

Tim Dlugos

Euphoria. Hitting crescendo. Bubble bursting in night. You wake
with bleeding eye. "Bleeding tears?" R asking. Incorrigible. Mid-
morning eyeball rouge et noir. Bus to doc in likely swish hood
—eye specialists chez nous oft smartly installed. Having
somehow opted out of public health. But bus stopping. At
ordinary midtown street. Red-brick old-style edifice. Modest
storefronts under. Elevator so dark. Fearing eyesight going

completely. Foyer, drab, narrow. Barely room for large woman, wheelchair. Hubby, in odd ensemble of army fatigues. As if on way to war. Squished in corner behind. Where emitting occasional loud sigh. They argue, noisy, persistent. Non-nonplussed everybody listening. Behind high counter, receptionist. Surrounded by piles of files. Coloured tabs. Many piles. So high, it seeming like comedy set. Elevator continually opening direct into foyer. Emitting men delivering boxes + boxes of pharmaceuticals. Via door to left. At exactly 2p. Called into office on right. Nice older doctor with older equipment. Giving efficient diagnosis. You profusely thanking—until she annoyed. For "taking at last minute." But no way you knowing of. To get doc appointment so expeditiously. Chez nous.

South Ferry bus. Put your card in slot, get receipt. To be *sans* receipt if uniform gets on. Is to pay $150 fine. Eminent North poet will have spoken of acquiescence in face of uniforms. In your own retrogressive way. Uniforms = Father = always nervous at border. Bus doors open. Uniform gets on. Your arm proffering, deferential, ticket. Such a good girl! Several other automatically submissive arms. Woman with Eastern European accent having none of it. Yelling whole system confusing. Plus not enough stops. + + +. Uniform de-boards [Guy-de-Bord]. At once sober rows of downcast eyes. Animated. Congratulatory. Chatting conspiratorially. From seat down aisle loud laugh. Black passenger [no longer absorbed in his book]. Laughing laughing. Laughing at

M. NourbeSe
Philip

all of us. Shaking with laughter, still. When Gail disembarking. Halfway to South Ferry.

SPLOTCH! Left cornice blackening. Like blot of ink. Spreading over table. Over delicious tagine + young Toronto writer. Complaining Gail [older generation] "having it all." On to BPC. Featuring iconic boomer poet. Today leaning on cane. Outside poetry club low scrubby front. Long grey braids. Loose turned up jeans. Long scarf, smoking. Performing older woman living/ writing life. And to-hell-with-post-stroke constraints. She laughing + we laughing with. That being meaning of Star. *Intégrale*, at one with one's work. Cane discarded, ushered onto stage. Reading something not quite to scratch. "That was a cliff hanger," she laughing. We laughing too. Out coming huge printed broadsheet, part of exhibit at Whitney. Long poem involving ancient Greeks, crab-stepping right up there on frieze of poet's dreams. She crinkling huge sheet in microphone: Paper riff to dead-leaf ancients. Enjoying. Crinkling again. Reading, she likes it; we like it. It *really* is terrific + we *really* do. A list-poem following: found things. Maybe less thrilling. But lesson in choosing from mundane everyday verbal detritus. Yet capable of floating or

> . . . *sliding like this down the long tilting hill*
> *Past the place to play and all the past*
> > *I saw the moon's*
> *Last quarter in the southern sky at dawn*

Speaking of tilted landscapes. Current *séisme* happening. On high floor of swank NYC hotel. But lower down in social body. Being that French IMF director DSK. Charged with hotel maid *sequestration/attempted rape*. The French, horrified. Their Socialist presidential hopeful photographed. Doing perp walk in handcuff. Sneering at "puritanical Americans." Wife *proud of [his seductiveness]* ... *It's important to seduce, for a politician.* In France great men not dissed. For personal proclivities. That being essence of word "French." USians countering [with unabashed hyperbole]. Ordinary Citizens treated equally in this country. DSK's expensive lawyers immediately investigating maid's private life. For dirt. On maid's side. Sharp young black prosecutor. Plus large crowd of hotel workers. Mostly women of racialized minorities. Outside courthouse shouting: *Shame on you.* Also, it being America—whiff of conspiracy. The whole thing orchestrated. By French right. To discredit rising Socialist Party candidate. But whether trial to take place debatable. For, notwithstanding alleged forensic evidence. Had not maid lied to immigration on entering country? Was not boyfriend in jail? Alas for DSK. Additional pesky annoyance of young writer. Back in Paris. Trying to take him to court. For attempted rape.

Descending steps. Into dark Lower East Side building. Finding self in bar. Thin woman. Elegantly dressed-down in casual American way. Saying: "Drink, it pays the rent." Down one more set of stairs. Up other side. Into theatre for panel of young women

Dominique Strauss-Kahn

prose writers. *The sentence wasn't English but it was language nonetheless. It used the Roman alphabet; it employed blank space to separate letters into various groups; and, most convincingly, the length of it ended with a period, that dot, that fleck of dust that ruins conversations.* You loving idea period a fleck. For if period "ruins conversation"—might it not also. If used in ways similar to line-end in poetic enjambment. Opening space. For reader input/invention? R, introducing little green detective chaplet *Moralia* on book table. Declaring: . . . "Gladman's supra-study has been the study of prose as an investigative poetic form in + of itself —not for example as prose poetry . . . Rather than 'experimental prose' a better name for Gladman's prose + our feminist prose community: PROSE. PROSE."

Gladman

Levitsky

In J's boudoir—space only for generous bed—pillow against frosted glass partition—INSOMNIAC sleeps. Sleeping. Sleeping. Dreams happening all round. Orchestrated by riverboat lamp base. By doll on shelf. Cat-faced shade. Crawling between sheets. Body sinking into arms of Morpheus. As if sex—whole anatomy leaning in. Once a week, round midnight. Real party. Voices, tinkling glasses, louder + louder as night passing, laughing, voices rising to shouting, someone screaming: "Put it out." Windows slamming shut. AC units set high. Not drowning racket. Abruptly, 4a, quiet. Subsequent Saturday, same story. R saying some people running after-hours clubs. In flats. To pay rent. Others running lucrative illegal hotels, you telling RG. Over delicious tagine, at

East 8th resto. Talk turning—in wake of Belladonna event. To question, *d'où on écrit*.... Question, at height of experimental feminist writing group chez nous [essentially identitary]. Now, for you. Writing subject composed, *rather*, of ventriloquized voices. Seen not as one 'person.' But in narrative patterns of multivocal resonance. RG saying for her part. Subject stepping *into* narrative. Implying subject locomotion. Until able to exert agency. Outside central station. Of story.

Days mesh, they rain. Washing piss smell off concrete. Trees turning leaves forward. To drink. Or away in repudiating wind. AC unit opposite adding soft persistent whine. Another somewhere churning/creaking. Like ancient lawnmower. Blending with ambient brouhaha. So that pores, entire body. Absorbing faintest environmental stimulus. Like those petal-faces abundantly fronting [walking West]. Greenwich dwellings. Their little faces turning this way + that. Catching sun rays floating upon breeze. You asking older male writer. You happening on in Greenwich. Friend of late William Burroughs. If old Beat having, as rumoured. Response-armoury at ready. In case of threat. Knives. Revolvers. Rifles. "Yes." "Was he kind?" "Very or else very not." Walking back East. Leaves blowing pleasantly. Your face also turning this way + that. Catching last rays. Piercing shadows.

Tropism—>in reverse: Flamboyant lawn-flower jacket. Worn by Conceptualist poet. For visit to White House. "Wallpaper" jacket.

Quipping late-night comic, Jon Stewart. Laughing Laughing. Purpose of jacket being to signal poet's brand of *uncreative writing*. A kind of fake-garden armour. Against external affect-stimulus. His students seeking to be expressive, creative, original. Corrected. To make way for poems constructed. Via induced or imposed constraints. You admiring Conceptualism's antecedents. For one, Oulipo's hyper-conscious re-structuring of haphazardly encountered spaces, memories, objects. But our little brain screens being already full. Of language bias. How much personal class/race/gender baggage going unexamined. In Conceptualism's rigourously procedural concatenations? Like it or not. Here is psychology again. *I might have once thought it was enough to reframe the language in order to shift the conversation to a discourse about network culture, but I keep intervening and so the text then fails over and over again,* writing RF in "Failure, a post-conceptualist poem." Fitterman

Evening in J's Museum. Pausing to enjoy terrific Latin music. From car window below. When last word on constraint from incomparable Blanchot. Tumbling by chance. Off shelf of book spines turned to wall. Volume called *Foucault/Blanchot*. Arguing constraint always already built in: *We are ever more subjected. From that* subjection, *which is no longer crude but subtle, we draw the glorious consequences of being* subjects *and free subjects capable of transforming the most diverse modes of a lying power into knowledge. We do this to the extent that we are CONSTRAINED TO FORGET its transcendence while at*

Maurice
Blanchot

the same time we replace a law of divine origin with various rules and reasonable procedures that, once we have tired of them, will seem to us to have come from a human—but monstrous—bureaucracy.

Coultas

Alternate poetic: Friend B setting tush on Bowery St chair. The better to be absorbing tatters of variegated raucous sonorities: *The Bowery plan goes something like this: there are explosions + condos arise Las Vegas-like from the smoke.* THAT'S THE MAYOR'S PLAN. Poet's plan being to sit . . . *at the same place and time for a season and participate and expedite street life.* For. Sitting or walking with B = Tuning into city's ghosts. Old bones of buildings. Imaginary walk-maps of late Allen Ginsberg, Larry Rivers. Or, today. Exiting subway onto 8th. Stunned by flapper-age NEW YORKER HOTEL. Stepped Deco heights. Geometric façade. Summoning [for noir-spellbound Northern] red-headed Raymond Chandler girls. Parading through fancy lobby. Sleight-of-hand gangsters. Waiting. In low shark-like vehicles. Idling soundless outside. Which luxe 2500-room monument. To Depression era excess. Boasting multiple big-band era ballrooms, restaurants, barbers for 42 chairs. Etc. Whereas for B. Façade calling up Tesla's lonely last 10 years. 33rd floor. Set-back Deco tower. Having failed to be accredited for pioneering role. In invention of electricity. Turning onto 34th. In search of 2nd-hand shops. Behind dense period façades. Their gorgeous architectural detail casting shadows. Over narrow street. Their once scrumptious insides gutted. Till only odd crown molding, or radiator grille. Or wall of marble tiles.

Whispering in dark. Was not Whitman, himself, saying: New York ever reconstructed. Being permanently in flux.

A restaurant on 9th. Run by young people. Named after said celebrated poet. For whom America *Centre of equal daughters, equal sons / All, all alike endear'd, grown, ungrown, young or old* ... Thin girl—thigh-high laddered stockings. Stepping from behind resto cash. To fetch beer sausage in kitchen. Cooking, classic Americana. Slow-cooked pulled pork, chicken. Mouthwatering, served on bread you can't eat. But holding sausage with caramelized onions. Carefully. In napkin. Dragging suitcase to laundromat on 1st. On high shelf by entrance. Two Buddhist altars. Half-eclipsed by loud large-screened, tanned, tattooed, Jersey Shore reality TV shenanigans. While sheets turning + tumbling [fingers crossed no bedbugs on folding tables]. Scooting round corner to gluten-free bakery. Muffins, carrot cake. And wonder of wonders: cute little cupcakes. Choosing corn muffin with jalapeno. Perfect with sausage. Walking home, 9th. Thoughts more dissimulated in folds of stomach. Than in labyrinthian folds of any poetics. After Whitman's. Local brewer. Then funky herborist. Small Mexican diner, home-cooked meals. Proprietors sitting inside. Waiting. Finally Cafe Pick Me Up's beloved bitter coffee. Middle-aged guy in Bermudas entering. Holding feather-weight burger. Downing 2 traditional Cokes out of bottle. Taking burger with to can. Frequented by continual stream from park opposite. Once. Being there. With Montréal

Whitman

students. Guy exiting restroom. Yelling someone at our table taking crap *sans* flush. Yelling yelling. Till all eyes focussed on red-faced kid. From chez nous.

Nina Simone round midnight. Ushering in sleep. Singing at Carnegie Hall. Broadway songs. Or angry southern blues. *Mississippi Goddam!* Other evenings, listening to strands of news. Rumble of street. Trace of neighbour music. Thoughts loosen, multiply. Ah, there's Michelle on screen. Smiling, confident. Inviting rappers. Spoken word artists. Poets of various stripes. To White House. [FURNITURE MUSIC playing North's Mr. SHHH. Offering *himself* as cultural event at official Prime Minister residence. Bent knee, foot pounding hard hard on floor, smashing out rock song on keyboard. Imagine sleeping with that?]

So are USians *really* more easily blending highbrow. And pop-cult. For which American genius globally acknowledged? Searching web for avant *poets*. Either invited to Obama White House. Or somehow, otherwise, briefly part of wider discourse. You finding Language Poet. On right-leaning Fox TV Bill O'Reilly's show. Being chewed out for teaching "anti-American" class. At Fordham. Poet for duration. Posting small smile. Neatly footworking with faint humour. Round O'Reilly's charges of anti-cap, American-hating rhetoric. Allegedly served up. To innocent students. Said poet. Also seen footworking. On Merce Cunningham dance studio floor. Located in classy elder

Bruce
Andrews

residence. Overlooking Hudson. Walking there. Further west than usual. Losing bearings on curvy West 4th. Older woman in grey jogging pants + flying grey hair. Who going right there. Adding [confidentially] 'we' not caring how 'we' looking at 'our' age. But at least arriving as aforementioned Lang-poet doing quick cross-step barefoot over floor. Red boxer shorts. Sign saying NUTTY PROFESSOR. Choreographed by poet's avant dance partner. Who torquing *West Side Story*. Into *uncodified, nonidiomatic shapes + rhythms of the body outside of canonized genres or codified vernacular.* The "West Side" boy dancers. Recast in Sally Silvers parodic same-sex pas de deux. Almost operatic female voice in background. Singing lines from Nutty Professor's "Reefer Madness" poem: "LICK, LICK, LICK / NO LICKING / DERELICDICTATION / DARE A LICK, DICK / DERELICDICTATION / NO LICKING." Andrews

Once more. Scarce week to go. Falling asleep. FURNITURE MUSIC fading into ironic patriotic dream. Several Citizens of Republic, standing on Union Square. Snickering at placards announcing WORLD ENDING TOMORROW. The sign-bearers scraggly to point of pathetic. Large woman, bright colours, thin orange tinted hair. Skinny pockmarked guy, etc. All sure to be disappointed on waking. Unless sign-holders not in fact devotees. Just paid with free meal [+ admonishment to repent]. Your dead uncle's screaming on phone, *Gail read Revelations!* Dreamtime, being like time of nostalgia. Transmogrifying—till you abruptly under beautiful thundercloud dusk. After mediocre Poetry Club reading. Walking amid other unsated poets. Toward compensatory Ukrainian food. The post-thunderstorm Manhattan evening sky billowing, grey-blue above. So peaceful. Notwithstanding 1st Ave traffic. The stuffed cabbage rolls. Delicious.

Dove Economics: Mourning doves outside J's Museum windows. First perceived cooing + complicit on iron balcony. Exemplary. Loving Couple. But soon, if male, with prettier rosy flush of breast. Leaning over flower pot of seeds to feed. Smaller scrappier female pecking his back. Pecking, pecking. Till he retreats. Or she simply sitting on seeds. So neither eating. Her whole little body filling entire circumference of flower pot. Maybe they just sucking up vibes of cut-throat town. Like urban sparrows. Who, it is said, singing badly. Cause miming ambient cacophony.

Heat rising, exponential. Gail ever sleepier. Someone saying unlike locals. Visitors lacking defence against racketous stress. Barking dogs on leashes. Garbage disposal vehicles. Idling cars. Loud people. In cab far downtown to meet potential US Publisher. Asking cabbie best route to follow. He naming streets of Moscow. You in dandy silk scarf. A scarf may be blasé. Or signify over-effort. Watching those girls rushing along Eastside sidewalk, bare necks, hair piled high to side. Tight little dresses, flashing toes [. . . *The dandy should seek to be sublime without interruption; he should live* Baudelaire *+ sleep in front of a mirror*]. Removing scarf. Publisher has long hair,

118

is beautiful. Two jobs. So not likely sleeping much. In front of mirror. Naturally

Penultimate date with R. Women's bar. Dumbo. Shadow of mammoth Roman arch. Seducing you 2 Lilliputians. Standing at bar. Scarfing sticky dates, sausage, cheese. Decent amounts of red. Scoping muscled women entering. Broad shoulders, fresh shirts. Damp just-showered hair. Outside-workers from port below. Type of girl we needing more of. You telling each other. Then to gallery for show *Recalculating*. Your 2 shadows now long. Against cinematic skyline of geometric cranes. Sundry warehouses. Bathed in warm damp breath. Coming up from water. Artist's work Technicolored, violent. Some from film noir stills. He either loves her. Or about to kill her. R reserving favourite cartoon-like woman sticking revolver out car window. You, across room, admiring painting called *Ruskin*. Ironizing truth-to-nature art. Being painted "recalculation" of time spent by artist + hubby. In British Columbia. **1970**s couple. Small + distant. Standing in stylized forest of leafless trees. Bare stylized arms of branches stiffly raised. Against sky full of hard autumn colour. Cat standing by woman. Tail likewise, tensely raised. You projecting own painful **70**s open "revolutionary" marriage. Inhabiting painting in toto. Exiting to street. Past woman on cement block. Pretty dress. Awaiting lover said to be abusive. And down street onto long grimy F-train platform. Again right out of American Noir tradition.

Susan Bee

With New Narrative cohort in from San Francisco. Talking not narrative. But break-ups. Which is talking narrative. Men fight

Glück

ritualistically, saying BG. There are codes. Women fight for right to be right. Studying menu with fantastic array of pierogis, blintzes, pancakes, waffles you can't eat, BG adding: You can see it with dogs. Strolling to reading up Park Ave South. Happiness extreme at thought of hearing experimental narrative. After régime of mostly poetry for month. Spacious row of 6th-floor gallery windows. Framing single black Montréal-style triplex. Squashed ghost-like below. Mid older office edifices. Extreme traffic noise flooding into gallery. With welcome evening breeze. Fanning S's *Sentimental Education*: Her fantastical cross-gendering youth. With sad bewildered Midwest Italian mother watching. Through schoolyard fence. *i became aware of my own mortality when I didn't think my desire could ever lead to other bodies until I found out about the man I would become, Pier Paolo Pasolini, whose body was found battered on wasteland near the sea.* But being girl, lacking same sustaining relationship to mother. As Pasolini, the son. *Pasolini + his mother were a couple; they shared a household until his death. To break their symbiotic relationship would have rendered her life force inaccessible to him but to sustain it required*

Szymaszek

sacrifice. When I became Pasolini, I could not abide by this conflict....

Then friend from San Francisco. Getting up + doing camp section from *About Ed*: Having been to see Dietrich in *The Devil is a Woman*. Now theatrically entreating her. To help re-invoke lover,

Ed. Dying of AIDS: *This is what Ed + I took from the film: In order to make the screen dazzle, Sternberg slid beads of glycerin down hundreds or thousands of invisible strings, slow rain . . . The roar of rain out of proportion to the slow movement of light, just as the roar of sex is out of proportion to Dietrich's indifference, or to the act of penetration, an imbalance that gave her a fairy tale passivity.* And Bob, a man having no trouble crying. Recounting, both drolly + sadly. How glycerine tears [plus lacy black parasol]. Providing fucked up image for mourning Ed. Ed, sincerely, deeply, mourned. Yet inescapably glossed by the glycerine drops. . . . to *make our love last forever?*

Glück

Again time to go? Last night, decamping to red-headed French woman's flat. Loving rigourous perfection of French interior. Crackling sheets. White sofa. Trees in front of spacious upper story windows. Cooling, *sans* air conditioning. You asking about DSK. She, tired of being French woman in NYC talking about DSK. No alarm clock. Having tossed $10 phone. Gail awake all night. Former fear of flying. Recycled to fear of missing plane. And what's a visit to New York. *Sans* one last cab? Actually, car service in older Lincoln. Air-conditioning full blast, passing though tunnel. Industrial Jersey moonscape. Toward airport. You asking Dominican driver about gas consumption. He segueing to cost of life. Subsidized apartment—3 bathrooms. Recent party for all the birthdays. Of all his children [you imagining the music]. Which children only now introduced. Because 3 different mothers. One, African. One, American. One, Dominican—the official one. Just now informed of others. How she taking it? *Right now she's very quiet.* He talking of missing home, the Dominican Republic. Too expensive to go. But hiring Haitian to build house. For his mother. Haitians, very poor. Dominicans hire Haitians [poster in La Cabane bar in Montréal warning not to vacation in Dominican Republic cause *500,000 Haïtianes y travaillent comme des esclaves*]. We getting onto subject of countless thousands of undocumented people. Living in New York. Some arriving in airplane mechanic uniforms. He knowing, for used to work at airport. He's been a Citizen for 12 years. He is happy to be a Citizen.

2012

CHELSEA ROUGE [SO YOU SAY YOU WANT A REVOLUTION]

Montréal, QC [**04.12**]: To have stood. Mid desultory corner loiterers. Cigs stuck on lips. Eyes vaguely shifting toward raucous Carrés-rouges demo. Wave. After wave. Red felt squares pinned to student bags. Fresh mouths scanding: *DOWN WITH NEO-LIBERAL IDEAS / RAS-LE-BOL DES IDÉES NÉOLIBÉRALES!* Causing tear of nostalgia. To be crevassing older lefty cheek. Were not your own youthful student protests likewise extending? To class-based social demand? And aren't they lovely, those flushed cheeks? Endearing dark eye circles. From nights of talking, smoking, painting placards. With slogans.... True, already

[**11.11**] Failing to get involved. Rushing down Broadway Ave. NYC. Nose running. Wind tearing scarf from ears. Dying to be feeling, smelling. Maybe entering Occupy Wall St encampment. Then finding some kind of barrier. Zuccotti Park tents stretching out behind. Your head, craning over tourists gathered there. Families with strollers. Plain clothes cops [being well-trained in discernment of that]. Trying to read titles on Peoples' Library table. Some poets you knowing. And Adorno. Who calling poets at once *last enemies of bourgeoisie + last bourgeois*. Standing there, it occurring. Older kidneys ill advised to be unrolling blanket. Sleeping on ground. Mid youth snuggling in sleeping bags. Some bags gently moving. One occupant saying: On entering camp, feeling WHOLE WORLD AT FEET. *I just started crying. I was like, this is not like anything I've ever seen. It's what we've always wanted to be happening but never figured out how to do.* Just back from working as model in London. They scorning critics of Occupy's anarchic lack of demands. *Demands will eventually come. But this is a space for learning. I've learned more here in the last 2 weeks than I have in all those years of college.* The struggle for/learning of—egalitarianism. In all its micro + macro forms. [But another sleeping there. On ground. Mornings crossing street. To advise financial institution on applying Occupy participatory democracy methods. To financial industry workplace. Company's CEO vaunting: *Our profits spiked immediately.*] Are not all revolutions spotted with unwitting betrayals....?

Stephen Boyer

[DEFENCE & ILLUSTRATION]

Stretched [**05.12**] on Chelsea Airbnb bed. Waiting for computer to charge. Ere fleeing to air-conditioned café. It being usual hot smelly NYC summer day. Cats' fleas proliferating in heat. Making of silky ass. Welted itching grid. Via open window, multivocal choir. Hens being raised in court below. By 2 [cop-expulsed] Occupy poets. The baseline chicken techno. Backing car horns. And morning brake-screech down West Ave, by Hudson. Planes. Landing. Squealers squealing. Melancholy sax. Trains. Construction racket. Crazy variety of birdsongs. Birds, symphonious. Compared to North backyard's scratchy sparrows. Starlings. Now, mockingbird. Just up from South. Along with warming clime. Trying some lady robin notes. Not bad. Not great. He doesn't care. Trying something else.

Message from North: *Gail come home! Here it's* [les Carrés-rouges] *revolution. And you in New York!* But, as in a dream. You just arriving from airport. The Chelsea brownstone, swish. Anomalous on opening door. To dim + cavernous atrium. Several feral cats. Half-flight up, blonde in flowing gown. Faint southern accent summoning tattooed dude, Sax. To be hauling luggage. Up silver stairs [small table statues of men on horses. Maybe (you projecting), Confederate steel soldiers]. Up black-painted flight. Up narrower black flight. Room, single bed slanting on floor. Gaping doorless closet. Stuff hanging out. GIANT chest of drawers. Corner, nice little desk. Indeed

Every room in house presenting as X-ray dream of detective novel. Once housing famous filmstar. Its elegant drapery drawn. To be revealing 2 habitants of Chelsea house common. That gorgeous pair of ex-Occupy youth. Just up from sewing praying mantis eggs. In garden. For eating up mosquitoes. Dyed black heads. Bent over little screen. At end of long table. Where North Carrés-rouges student revolution. Expanding into hoods. Massive parade of elders. Toddlers. Hipsters. Tender adolescents. Thronging street upon narrow Plateau-Mont-Royal street. Banging *casseroles*. The dimming salon light. Grazing youths' hair. And mod apparel. Inferring faint congruence with mansion's exquisite tiling. Tiffany-style chandeliers. Delicate carved woodwork [Italianate or Greek Revival] windows.

Woman on stairs. Absent for days. *Feverish*. Her mate explaining. Having marched entire scorcher-of-a-May-1-demo. In latex Miss Piggy regalia. Now. Abruptly re-appearing. Lovely. Erect. In wingback Queen Anne salon chair. Mid toys. Papers. Cords. Electronics. Little table. Bags of bagels. Cat stuff. Leaning over. She selecting piece of crinkly paper, from box. And attaching to curls. Presto: a sunflower. Little child, big glasses. Hidden behind book. Emitting, from time to time, small animal sounds. Outside long windows. Trees bending. Heavens instantaneously darkening. One of frequent intense storms. During canicule in city. Child pushing chair to open window. Feet outside, despite violence of elements. "Don't fall," mother offering mildly.

Like all these amazing tree houses and pirate ships
You are building with your mind and on paper
Rooms attached with ladders suspended spiraling

Around masts or trunks

Ask what anything is and I will

Tell you you say   Ingenious inventions in

Rooms to house the energies of our new habitations   Brown

Adjoining twin ceiling-high salon window. Sporting bullet hole.
Staunched with packing tape. In memoriam of [1970] shooter.
Climbing roof opposite. To be firing at quietly dining filmstar.
Whose almost-murder said occasioned. By calling, on TV talk
show. For US rapprochement with China.

Climbing to room [pleading allergy to cats + their fleas].
Preferring, like any Northern. To be alone. Pulling sheets, black
[why black?]. To chin. To be fending off vermin. A little hungry.
Having buried salmon from fine corner grocer. Deep in fridge's
cornucopia of Trader Joe dumpster gleanings. Courtesy of
ex-Occupiers. Stepping out nights with shopper carts. And
gathering usable grocer discard. For common use. Thus, laying
there in top-floor bed. You savouring, instead, hometown *Le
Devoir* coverage of Carrés-rouges uprising: *Le gouvernement will
not resolve this student conflict as long as it fails to grasp that it is dealing
with a generation not like other generations, a generation whose goals
excede the education issue, + whose protest is not likely to stop any time
soon*. Then dream

Cut. To choked L-train platform. French sweater, pearl buttons,
bloused   in   at   waist.   Albeit.   Notwithstanding   Frenchy

presentation. Gail less Baud-type [show-off] dandy. Than *Poe-type*, a-social. For whom to be alone meaning. To be *dissimulated* in crowd. [*The harder a* (wo)*man is to find, the more suspicious* (s)*he becomes.*] Who now disappearing. Into St Mark's. Not usual Poetry Project Parish Hall reading locale. But actual Church Sanctuary's elegant plain [Protestant] lines. Muted. Beige. White. Pews packed with congregants. From avant jazz/poetry milieux. Already in thrall. To John Zorn horn-ordained exaltation. For all free musical improvisation —tilting toward religious in tone. Now. Cacophony referencing. In reverse time order. Brouhaha outside your Chelsea early morning window. Planes. Honking. People screams melancholy train wind rushing traffic in loud tunnel crazy high bird boat-horns, fight-boos in football field loud buses, bird high-wire. Music. Acknowledging its sources. Simultaneously deep in convo with Thurston Moore Fender amp. Crowd increasingly akimbo, eroticized: To *paw* is to possess [a gesture of loners?]..... *We are all mutants in our own gaze* ... —calling out young poet EK. Long black curls, faux-leopard top.—..... *let's hang the used condom on a branch / of an olive tree   let's ask one less question // at the end of each chapter &read.* . . . Then long tall poet from Cincinnati. Thin arm, pointed finger, rising from lectern. Like fragile pale-stemmed winter plant. A skeleton speaking of . . . *my skeleton.* Which *floats alone and singing.* Then a poet voicing musical composition of multiple tongues *dancing together.* Shouting down in avalanche of languages—notably Indigenous:..... *hegemonic forces.* . . . *[In]*

poems so fierce, fraught, bladey and mobile. [Their] . . . showiness and
flaunt. . . . are like the fierceness of the drag balls Diggs salutes in one
poem: a visible weapon, a tactic simultaneously offensive and defensive,
a wargame for the whole body. Dream

Joyelle
McSweeney

Set. Now resto. Somewhere on 6th. Where Gail *cafardant* to
R, she hungry. On account of looking repeatedly. For own
personal BUTTER, PEANUT BUTTER, BREAD, FISH. In common
fridge. Either gone. Or buried irretrievable. In refrigerator
depths. R to reply: "*IT'S* [i.e. the Chelsea house] *A GOOD PROJECT!*
You just needing to get in step. With positivism of era. Put up
a sign: *I HEART YOU. BUT DON'T TAKE MY SHIT.*" Your resto
table. Already cleared of shared sparse antipasti, prosciutto di
Parma, salame Toscano, crotonese, mortadella, focaccia.
Craving more. Outside window. Shorebird profile of well-known
author [*Haunted Houses*]. At terrasse table. Plus your NYC
publisher. Earlier saying you lucky to be launching *Obituary*
novel. With cool younger gay poet. Who, for sure, drawing
crowd. R saying your problem maybe age. You saying you're
making me cry. Tears glistening [a little glycerine]. In
carlights. You crossing avenue to ATM. On account of R's
preferring cash-only restos. "That's why no state health care
system in this country." You snapping. She kindly offering
prose work as present. Page opener: *Since I have been at the*
Benjamenta Institute I have already contrived to become a mystery to
myself.

Lynne Tillman

Robert Walser

Progressing down house hall. Weekends seeming darker. More cavernous. In contrast to bright sun outside. Leaking through thick panes. Sufficiently to distinguish prominent angles of furniture. Antique, well-used. Not to say, worn. And musical instruments, scattered. As if St Mark's concert having in fact. Begun here. Abruptly abandoned as people. En masse exiting. Perhaps to diner. For good American breakfast. So that you, standing there. Struggling to discern remote corner movements. Or any acoustics. From other rooms in house. Generally pretty silent. Notwithstanding number of inhabitants. Save loud last-Sunday lovers' quarrel. Breaking out on 3rd. Male voice shouting, vast clouds of pot smoke seeping under door. Eventually calming. Then all day. Strange woman. Pale, slim black clothes. Fab curly hair. Sitting alone at table. As if no place to go to. Later, joined. By child with glasses. Nose still in book. Said to be eating only round things: peas corn blueberries etc. You making comment on balanced diet. Mother saying. Not wanting to "bully them." Father adding: "Pizza definitely one of five food groups."

For new novel launch, Gail wearing tomato red cotton sweater. In solidarity. With hometown Carrés-rouges rebellion's unprecedented force. And numbers. And acts of direct democracy. Publisher finding garment too orange. Friend whispering, embarrassed: "Black is your colour." Mercifully, Chelsea house poet providing relax-potion Rescue. Excellent, mixed. With certain amount of alcohol. Cool gay poet reading first. Poem re: metaphorically fucking. Already systemically-fucked dead US soldier. Himself, by definition. Systematically fucking some other nation's soldier. Reading, reading. Near whole hour. Till half of audience eclipsing into night. And you, in your dream. Into darkness of Tompkins Square park. Where happening upon star of *Big Bang Theory*. [Vaguely resembling aforementioned poet.] Doing some complex computer thing. Very friendly. Till he. Utra-impeccable germophobe. Very shiny hair. Noticing your hoody. Kind of smudged. Still, you 2 ending up [this often happening]. Back in Montréal railway flat room. Lots of empty shelves.

Today. Gail is wearing French New Wave cinema-style pale green linen top. Large buttons. Flat collar. For poet *Rob's Word Shop* in Bowery Poetry Club window. He behind glass. Close shaven face [+ head]. Very impeccable shirt, tie, suit. Who, like Bartleby, the scrivener. Preferring not to be expressing own subjectivity. So that ... *Instead of accepting commissions for creative writing, [he] merely transcribed words at his costumer's request and charged them for a task they could have easily accomplished without intercession. Ironically, given the sales of poetry (especially that of avant-garde poetry), Fitterman's* Word Shop *probably "moved more product" than many poets.*

Derek Beaulieu

This window makes me feel like a groupie but not, I hope, a dishonest one—my only real agenda is to bring awareness into the American consciousness. This window makes me feel like how

many parents and teens see no connection between God's word
preached on Sunday and the decisions they make during the week.
This window makes me feel like the taboo goes too far in not
allowing for exceptions. This window makes me feel like I'm
immersed in reality and it's a good thing that I can still dream and

Fitterman
fly. This window makes me feel like it's payback time.

Now. Huge brown *material* bird. Flapping by long Chelsea
window. While on laptop, on long common table: Talking heads
of Montréal Anglo media. Vigourously excoriating violent late
night Carrés-rouges direct democracy. Then Franco reporters
coming on. Lauding dissident crowd as peaceful. Even in
diverging from city-licensed route. Under mostly tolerant eye of
cops. Gail, seated under table's Tiffany-style chandeliers.
Sermonizing North 'revolution.' To whomever available: 1)
Visiting leader of Belgian Pirate Party. 2) Two Californians
importing medicinal herbs native to Americas [cause cheaper in
China]. 3) Young Occupy lawyer taking City of New York to
court. For destroying People's Library at Occupy encampment. 4)
Young CUNY prof who with several members of his union
travelling to Montréal. In solidarity. All pausing to listen a
moment to Gail. Before rejoining mad race for survival. In
evermore crowded expensive conglomerate. Median income for
lowest-paid workers. Down $463. To $8,844.... Some 19,000
children in shelters. Luxury commerce thriving. Perfume. Autos.
High-end dining. Is not any foreigner loving [fearing] US
capacity. For exuberant excess.... *self-esteem exists and matters; can*

Chris Kraus
one be American without it?

Speaking of exuberance. Walking with B. Passing Disneyland-ish Economy Candy's neon window promise of sugar high. Brashly jumbo red-+-white peppermint pinwheels. Exuberant jars of large multi-pastel-toned gumballs. *CHOCOLATE BLOWOUT SALE*. Bulk Halva. Old Coke signs. Licorice/toffee bags. Bacon mints. Original CANDY BURGER. Made of 22 delicious bonbons. Licorice of every imaginable shade, since **1937**. What dose of confidence? Or entitlement it taking? To push sugar so casually. To such excessive heights.

Very next day. Coming upon film clip. Of old baroque ballet performance. Wherein Stein's *4 Saints in 3 Acts* [Virgil Thompson composer]. Playing in continual loop. At tony Met's Stein/ Picasso show. Performance's [**1934**] all-black male cast/choir in tutus. Not 4 but 20 saints lined up to dance. Posted near exit from exhibition. Of extensive museum Stein family art collection. Sign saying Steins NOT RICH! *Au contraire* [Inner Bolshevik barking]. And you recalling story of Stein pater familia. Pulling train emergency brake. When daughter's hat flying out window. Our Northern shocked. At that.

It is above all young SB, former Occupy resident poet. Who seeking news of Carrés-rouge struggle. And keeping Gail informed. Re: local demos of solidarity with Carrés-rouges students. When not working in basement, with partner. On huge Occupy poetry anthology. Offering Gail on departure. Magnificent present of enormous paper version of same. Volume wrapped in pink tissue paper. Black velvet ribbon. Featuring:

Poets from around the world [who] have been sending poems to the People's Library in an effort to create a living/breathing poetry anthology in solidarity with the Occupy Wall St movement. All poems are accepted into the anthology. Volume, too big for bags. To be posted. Never reaching Montréal. For which you feeling terrible. But here, an Occupy poem from digital version, *AMERICAN MARXIST*:

Chris Butters

> ... *I don't look like a Marxist,*
> *making my way*
> *not through Russia*
> *or Germany or France,*
>
> *but America,*
> *crazy America,*
>
> *juggling marriage, children*
> *mortgage, union,*
> *even as I seek*
> *a working class revolution*
> *in the belly*
> *of the beast.*
>
> *I get in the car*
> *and drive down Route 23*

TO BE: A FLOOD
[YOU KNEW IT WOULD COME]

Film Forum for *Céline + Julie Go Boating*. At which crucial
moment of our story. R coming down sidewalk. Little late. Under
ominous grey-white sky. Direct into movie. [Popcorn. But no
butter. For svelte New Yorkers.] One girl pursuing another.
Skinny Parisian legs running through streets in chunky heels.
Then *reverse*: first girl turning + running after other. Pair ending
in boat on Styx-like river. Other boats with ghosts of females
[their dead mothers, locked in male gaze]. Floating by. NO—the
Styx scene, rather, PRECEDING girls' reversal of pursuit. For girls
floating on river not dead. Simply making U-turn. Marking radical
reversal, for each from object to subject. A PALINDROME, R
saying. In her usual quick-thinking offhand perspicacity. You
identifying with city. One could also say—as **1970**s Belgian
feminist philosopher putting it—*A … regressive/progressive
liberation. Wherein two women unearth a law allowing their pleasure,
their desire. Their past being* [in the film] a house *"rue du Nadir-
aux-Pommes"* into which the young women drift from time to time.
The better to watch *two ladies* [their mothers] *fight over an
unfaithful man.* But daughters *escaping this classic female trap* … You
liking push-pull nature of girls' relation. Their reciprocal pursuit.
Functioning something like poetic enjambment. Its reverse-tread
movement neither totally disjunctive. [Faint narrative being
hidden somewhere therein.] Nor, yet, obsessively contiguous.

Françoise Collin
(trans. Scott)

137

Which movement also marking certain type of love. Wherein reciprocity *en principe*—the operative word. Here, we abruptly arriving

Back at beginning of our ramble. Just as Gail exiting West Village room. In dance producer's **1970**s artist-subsidized pseudo-deco flat. Its castoff sofa, mats, ungainly homemade pottery lamps. In rapid trot, to nice lunch at Frankie's. Favorite sausage, polenta. Those stewed prunes. With mascarpone. Any Northern knowing to eat warm. If weather cool. Your ex-Carrés-rouges table companion. In city on student visa. Energetically dissing [in adorable accented English]. *Sous-politicisation* of fellow NYU prime-tuition journalism students. If, in class, she getting "angry about politics." Southern girl trying to comfort. For feeling bad that day. Not much liking, either, that "progressive guy ok with making guns from 3-D printers." But you both ruefully allowing. Over coffee. Les Carrés-rouges already abandoning collective struggle. Contra neo-liberal ideas. For gov promise to freeze tuition. *After doing it for some time, for years and decades, the habit of protest becomes something else, something apart from, almost irrelevant to, one's initial desires. It becomes, to say it simply, a way of life. Or, to be more accurate if less simple: one's initial ambitions regress into merely a way of living.* . . . Such as

Sitting. On paisley sofa. Under **70**s wall-poster flautists. Reclining on leafy branches. Half-concealed by huge eye-patterned peacock tail. Itself submerged. In poster-glass reflection. Of 19th century water-barrel tower. On building opposite. Reaching to skyline. Conjuring early 20th era. When workers still knowing to struggle. For purpose of abolishing plus-value labour. Too bad that future perfect will have proved irreducible. To this [dreamed-of] economy. On adjacent living room TV. Barack Obama. Said to be LAST BULWARK. To rising continental right. Face grey, strained. Being in process of flubbing first **2012** TV election debate. Re-pub opponent Mitt Romney "looking like movie star." E noting, glumly. His Norman-Rockwell-style campaign. All about grit, religion, work. In face of O's alleged 'Euro'-style heavy social spending. And alleged failure to grasp. What making America great.

Implacably heavy sky. [But cool blue string of lights draped from top of building opposite.] In gesture of resistance.—Gail [Anaïs] walking *to the window flings it wide remembering a similar gesture made by Elizabeth Taylor and Alice B. Toklas. . . . . Her action throws resentment to the wind. . . .* And to the chatty pigeons.   Harryman
Happily composting on sill. And to the **70**s mock 'brothel'-style lamp, rust-colour shade. Stuck in back of ceramic turtle. Providing red-lit accoutrement. To traffic drone below. And jazz bar horns. Somewhat filtered by dark-brown-aluminum-framed window. But nothing drowning eternal tinny living-room TV. So stepping out again. Subway to Bryant Park. Exiting wrong side. Unable to find, in now streaming downpour [+ embarrassingly

streaming nose]. Poet JK. Who texting from some *other* park corner. Soaked to the bone. You 2 taking refuge. In plastic-smelling department store cafeteria. Where Gail [for a change]. Not obsessively parading inchoate grandparent-Indigeneity. As proof of solidarity with racialized people. Instead asking poet question you earlier putting to R. Over delicious Ethiopian stew. In Brooklyn bodega. [Are not 'people like us' loving food traditions from starving nations?]: WHY IS THE AVANT POETRY SCENE CURRENTLY [**05.12**] LACKING IN RACIAL DIVERSITY? R, answering. As per. With question: "And why do we never talk about it?" Sitting on plastic bench of cafeteria, drying off. JK venturing it may be getting worse.

> You are the affirmation of the plural cause.
>
> You are the angel gliding between histories
>
> you must use and ones that silence you,
>
> man, African, American, Harvardian, human.
>
> Amid this desert of touch, threadbare
>
> society of friends who can never
>
> truly comprehend or love you

Keene

2nd [**2012**] electoral debate. Difficulty breathing. What if Obama again bested. By hawkish, environmentally-indifferent, socially Conservative Repub Romney? Gallons of ginger tea to open bronchials. Nearly pissing on sheet. The President. And wife Michelle. Gorgeous in tailored pink. Simple string of pearls. Most elegant White House pair since Kennedys. He having in first debate deployed ... *presidential decorum to a Xanax extreme,* now

tucking *away a dinner of steak and potatoes and then . . . out on stage*
with plenty of red meat for anxious supporters. Chest to chest.
Disputing. Filibustering. Toward win. We, the many, now glued. Peter Baker
Joyful. To moment. Impervious to tropical wave moving off
western coast of Africa. Into eastern Atlantic. Whose indifferent
nature to be seeding future turmoil [ultimately political]. In
overheated ocean.

Rain. Rain. More rain. Boarding crosstown bus in downpour.
Heading to St Mark's Parish Hall. Eager for poetry curator
S's warming full-body hug. The feeling of being loved.
Extraordinary in this circle of poets. Clinging together. As if
poets in this land clearly knowing. Who the enemy is. And what
dangers maybe coming. The Right. The planet. But can these NY
poets—you wondering again? Ploughing through crowd of poets.
Toward warm embrace of S. Can these poets. Living their small
group existence? Be in reality impacting wider public thinking?
In corner of eye, S. Leaning into long embrace of B.
Simultaneously quipping over B's shoulder: "This good time to
ask her to serve on the board?" Behind podium, tiny poet M
—huge scarf, hair upswept, reading—line by disjunct line. Yet
somehow totally not disjunct at all. Her words being pasted [in
your head] on little banners all over town.

That year dress supposed open-source
stenciling onto fabric as in the manner of

EXHAUST Welish

Also coating sidewalks, hair. Even windows of New Jersey born dance-producer landlady's flat. Where you, avant artist. Living 2 long months. Sans getting to know OLDER sister progressive. De facto survivor of terrifying McCarthy 50s. Surmounting great odds as female producer. Of important show billings. Whose exhausted gray curls now sinking nightly. Into beige sectional sofa cushions. Under gaze of Obamas. Peeking from postcards in kitchen alcove. In thanks for major fund-raising abilities. Which producer kindly inviting you. To New York City Center's Fall for Dance festival. Entering Center's neo-Moorish interior. Complete with ornate arabesque ceiling. Exquisite blue, gold, ivory tiling. Gracious curved stage. And 2 expensive little girls. Velvet ruches, long long curls. Patent leather shoes. Almost Victorian. Running up + down stepped auditorium aisle. As if part of set. As far as show. Producer liking classic ballet dancer's slender rendition. Of painful romantic trouble. Graceful in strapless, knee length tulle. Tender pink. A fragile thing. About to be jilted by her man. We feel her pain. Pain requiring no explicative program notes. Cause background narrative— everybody knowing. *The speaking voice of the lyric Ego* (being) *one*

already written. You arguing for another dancer's wild pointedly metallic gestures. Loud bar-type music. Jarring electric guitar. Stripped-down improvisational. Offering haptic take, you arguing. On female-Citizen artist. Home through Times Square. Building walls lit up. Ghoulish colours. Flashing cartoon lettering. Violent yet familiar. After Center's time-lapsed Moorish-revival interior.

[FURNITURE MUSIC's playing Dad's codpiece of a Masonic apron, his Masonic medals' strange symbols. He refusing to discuss. All tucked away in secret box. Even Mother not allowed to touch. You + adolescent girlfriend. Lounging on Masonic Lodge parapet. In largely French-Catholic town. Where Protestant Masons seen as ridiculous. Boldly lipsticked. Smoking.]

Today. God's breath so faint—leaves barely a-flutter. Sky weirdly white. Silence of trees suspended, breathless. Birds no longer singing. No jays to complain. No coo of white pigeon. No mocky slide-y starling choir in foliage. On iPhone, gigantic swirly maelstrom [cunt-hole in middle]. Roiling in from ocean. Standing watching Hudson River bloating. Every molecule bright + swelling, creating white-lit surface. Very dark under. Strange feeling in stomach. In little Village square, elaborate Hallowe'en -costumed children partying. Comme si de rien n'était.... Old rock songs blasting from sound system, audible for blocks. Drowning weatherman's report. Which report. To you, totally a poem:

. . . Lion's share of guidance
Indicating circulation associated with Hurricane S . . .
becoming incorporated into hybrid vortex
over mid Atlantic . . .
. . . high degree of blocking from Eastern North America (+)
entire Atlantic basin to allow

. . . unusual merger . . .

. . . (+) once the combined gyre materializes

. . . settling back toward the interior northeast

through Hallowe'en. Inviting

(A) . . . cyclone along the lines of "FRANKENSTORM"

Mary Shelley's Gothic creature of synthesized elements.

Guy on sidewalk near river. Will have been thinking to move car. Then letting stay put. Two previous panic-forecast hurricanes. Having skirted city. You deciding to do same. Till K on phone commanding: "Get out while you can." Not to be stuck with writing notes, computer. In chaos of public shelter. Scant hour later. Through empty streets. Serendipitous last taxi [yours]. Rising in arc over closing bridge. A . . . *curled woman on motorcycle / another waiting for her—on span ahead // —separated from*

Scalapino

Lydia Davis

one's—thorax. . . . At first land seems *flat and even when a hurricane . . . advancing over it.* In eerie breathlessness: Buses. Subway trains. Screeching to halt under bridge. Ere flooding entering tunnels. Tree branches, trunks. Torquing toward ground in sudden blast. Taxi pulling up to refuge on highest Brooklyn slope. Friend's hand, careful. Pouring wine. Stirring squash risotto. Monster outside. Not quite believable. Streaming on screen over city. Over shore communities. You eat. You kiss. You drink. Not wet, not cold. No power failure. No smoke or fire. Only backyard decades-old 2-story thick vine curtain. Aviary for marvellous + varied choir. Wind-flung to ground. From perch, you 2. Looking down on power poles a-shorting. Entire blocks afire. On screen, Manhattan blackout to 39th.

to wound the autumnal city.
    So howled out for the world to give him a name.
    The in-dark answered with wind,
    All you know I know: . . . . ,   Delany

All measure being relative to circumstance. How often are authors of lesser mettle than Delany. Able to make mere description of life. De facto estranged, torqued, reversed. Into what we calling *art*? Is it art to recount ghostly millions November-chilled. Walking wet. Their long-dead batteries. The poet bikewheels. Swishing over flooded pavement. Rare variety store candle flicker. Nouns flickering like candles on dimlit poetry student faces. Verbs gesturing from flood-swamped places. Named Breezy Point. The Rockaways. Red Hook. From Staten guillotine of student neighbour. Who entering garage as power flickering on/then off. And door plummeting down on neck. Another student . . . *casual* . . . Losing "everything except my hard drive. But my parents are middle class. We'll be okay." Just needing to depart workshop early cause: "We have flashlights, but at night if you walk about on Staten, vandals steal your batteries." Or K's apartment 16 floors up, Manhattan. Where for weeks shit cannot be flushed. Dark smelly stairways, corridors, maybe dangerous. When at last, lights go on, East Side project dwellers to be cheering. "As if Yankees winning World Series. . . ." Will it have been the poets. Who most profiting from disaster?

Candles in the kitchen, fat no. 2 pencil on exam blue books—that dark & none of electronic this made me write like hell. Aloneness and quiet in a long dark apartment where Leo was there on the Myles *other end with dogs and cats. Power comes on & writing stops.*

In devastated Repub New Jersey. Dem candidate Obama turning up. To comfort. Re-pub Romney does not. Sealing, some saying, Dem's chances in state. Where another poet hunkering down . . . *8 days without lights or heat. . . . so cold . . .* but *shelters don't take animals* (cats) *. . . plunged ontologically into a space not unlike that of my 19th century novel, cooking by candlelight, huddling under blankets and warming ourselves by the stove, rising to the metaphorical cock's crow. I took it as a sign* (for) *. . . this book . . . getting it out of my* Keene *(thinning) hair.*

*

Before all that. Gail, crossing dark Churchyard. Scoping skeletal poet. Stepping from darkest graveyard side. Enhanced whiteface. Framed in black kerchief tied back. Slim black dress down to ankle. One could say death figure. Predicating coming wounded city. Long black-clad body gently rocking. Reading rape jokes to mostly female audience. Culled on the net. Her art, poet to be declaring, creating own trap. Wherein to *stand . . . and wave, and often get caught. . . . To me, that's more illuminating than acting as if I could stand outside of the trap, or fashion the frame.* You, ever obsessed with how to write that estrangement. *Necessary* to radical upheaval. Fascinated. Then seeing young woman beside. Open-mouthed, in shock. Pale as if to faint. Other mouths in downward-dog grimace. Or posting faintly drawn ironic smiles. Perhaps Conceptualist. In tearing object [sexual assault] from interpretive frame. And context. Achieving desired shock effect. Yet, one could also ask. Is the poet not inadvertently re-(ag)gressing? By isolating object from its social relations? *No Language is Neutral.*

Near publisher's. Man awaiting bus in streaming, icy, lower-town Northeaster. Soaked to the bone. Droopy broken umbrella. Bulging worn-out briefcase. On way to cheap hotel. His lower Manhattan digs destroyed. In rising waters. No friends or relatives. Looking hopeful at your friendliness. Then withdrawing back into contemplative hole. As you choosing seat across aisle. The better to be thinking how to write moment [guy/rain/loneliness/general lack of empathy]. In *sentencing* of multilevel cadence. Lending this bus-estranging moment. Some kind of alternate grid. For narrative. Sitting there, you contentedly the artist. While knowing needy guy across aisle. Thinking you unkind. Or—as Québécoise friend declaring in her matter-of-fact Franco way: "To write is to betray."

In rain with poet B. Your savant ex-Midwest Baptist-raised locator. Of simple pleasures, bemusements. In lower city. Today air being sooty, low gray nimbi. Hunching instead on tiny bench. Under low tin-pressed ceiling of West-side café. Good salad, fried egg bacon bits on top. Guy beside's leg against yours [feigning reading book]. You opening page of B's new ms. To poem enigma of female friendship: *A girl promised a purse filled with jewels, if I would be her friend / Purses open secrets as priceless as pills in a jeweled box* ... Word 'secrets' moving 'friendship' from lyric ego [that which already spoken]. Toward what B, in her calm, astute way. Suggesting as procedure. For commissioned literary 'conversation.' Between the 2 of you.

GAIL + BRENDA GO BOATING

Brenda: What does Gail mean by choosing *The Obituary* as a title for her novel? Can an obit be written about the living? Who is dead or is this a collective obituary? List of survivors? Viewing hours? Funeral home? Cremation or burial? Where may I send the flowers or a blanket of garlands for a grave? A spray of roses and baby's breath or ceramic angels. . . . ?

The dead are not ghosts in Emily Dickinson's persona poems. Yet, they are aware that they have passed over and exist in eternity: Gail's ghosts, unaware of their own decease, live continuously in the present and inhabit a psychic dream state. They reside near the point where the currents of language, French, English and other tongues clash and converge like the

Saint Lawrence and Ottawa rivers thus generating power. The language is abridged, misheard and morphed by an immigrant's tongue and ear of Anglo with Québécois, and other tongues; perhaps the most hard to trace is the native tongue of the Indigenous bedrock beneath the European overlay of the Anglo and the Franco.

Gail: Brenda + I have ghosts in common. Like Brenda's, my ghosts creep up through the floorboards of language. Via a cutting + re-arranging of material objects into *ostensibly* seamless sentences/lines [fake narrative]. Brenda writes in *The Marvelous Bones of Time*: *Daniel Grass, the first white property owner in this area, killed by arrows*. The coincidence of the name "Grass," and "the first white property owner" is quintessential-Brenda: excavation + juxtaposition. Provoking sudden little flashes of light. There can be no identitary (re)-claiming here. Where Brenda writes "I am a color that is an uneven beige ... ," I write "suspect as the colour beige ..." Beige is the colour of uncertainty; Brenda's narrator would be seen as an "old whitey" along river border of former slave state. Across from which she growing up. She asks in a beautiful tough two-way sentence: "... are there any abolitionists hanging from my family tree?" *The Obituary* is for the dead mother. And her [said] lost Indigenous culture. Grandma Métis, claiming Grandpa [after she gone]. However, no indication she speaking the Métis language, Michif. Which language deploys its ghosts openly ... a combination of French/Cree, mostly. In the phrase "Aen sóré ayáw dan la cáv" [There is a mouse in the cellar] one can hear both Indigenous + French language traces. Speaking of reciprocity. Michif deploys Indigenous-language verbs [notably, Cree]. With French nouns. Two tongues perpetually in conversation. We don't hear presences until something leads us to think about them.

B: The architecture of her novel, *The Obituary*, is based on the structure of a Montréal triplex. Like a Brooklyn brownstone but with an outside staircase. *Railway-flat arched double decorated with plaster-leafed scrolling. Butt-dowelled ceiling angels.* Me, a straight reader who loves *The Obituary*, a channelled collaborative text told by a lesbian (maybe commie) historian, a fly, and keyhole peepers. *The Obituary* is loaded with gas, that is farting. Deflating frontier dreams of Paris on the prairie? Rude as New Amsterdam or New York? An imitation of European culture and capital? Very astute political observations: fart = PET = initials for Pierre Elliott Trudeau. After the snowstorm, walked to Tompkins Square Park in the afternoon.

G: There is snow in Tompkins Square Park. And in Montréal, now. In winter. *Not enough.* I am nostalgic for our brightly lit clear cold winters. Now degenerated into soupy mix of wet. Instead of soft, dry snow—we getting slush + "potlid" gray sky. I will soon be envying this Boston winter's mammoth blizzards. I already have poet envy. Such as the easy jump-cut that gets Brenda's journal musings in a heartbeat. From, say, farts in a Montréal stairwell. To NYC's Tompkins Square Park snow. Though her *Marvelous Bones* is mostly written in sentences—somehow the surface of the accidented landscape is made of language both disrupted. And rolling narratively. Like a freshly plowed field I love the tension between the narrative pull. And poetic language's spacey vectors. Trying to replace plot with overlapping perceptive frames. As she + other poets do. I used the triplex as a site where time comes + goes. In no particular sequence. If the inner staircase of my tale is heavy with flatulence. It is not due to the traditional high calorie diet [say, fèves au lard, tarte au sucre]. For combatting winter cold. The flatulent Québécois student hacker in my *Obituary* stairwell. Has been eating good old North American hotdogs. He is also farting to block out his condescending [+ reeking because dead] European French gendarme instructor. Kneeling 7 steps up at Rosine's room keyhole.

B: Considering the role of memory in composing poetry or fiction, there's a writing exercise called a rapid autobiography, in which one writes in, say 15 mins, the story of her life. Gail told me a story about her grandfather, a tea leaf reader, and how he saw death in the cup. And he was right, the son of the subject of the reading died, skating on a pond. And her grandfather was too distraught to ever read tea leaves again. Thinking about the things/events in early childhood that I cannot remember. Around age 4, I was playing hide-and-seek and fell on my grandma's wooden porch, busting my lip clear up to my nose. I was told that it took 32 stitches to close it. Must have been traumatic for my parents and siblings, but I can't recall any memory of it. Until I was about 18, I never looked anyone in the eye, and I wonder if this had to do with stitches and deep scar that remains even though I love my scar because it's a part of my story of being in the world, not to mention that it makes me look fierce. My oldest sister tried to kill a snake in the hay with a pitchfork; instead, she pinned my foot to the floor. Can't remember that, nor being chained to a pole by older sisters when they were supposed to be watching me.

G: It is perfect that Brenda forgets the scar incident entirely. Yet wears the sign of it so beautifully. New Narrative writers have made this failure to remember into a mantra. A performance, aggrandized. Manneristically. After excavating childhood for a novel or story, writers are often surprised to find that the childhood now remembered. Is the one in the book. Not quite real, not quite fictional. I have memories about hair. My once fair curls that my dark-haired mother cherished. A hairbrush on a little table. I know that as soon as my mother finishes talking to her sister—my daily torture will begin. Transforming me into the little ringleted princess for the adoring aunts. This way of time bringing threads together into focused material space. Then dispersing is one where I feel kinship with Brenda's accidented landscapes, rural or urban. Her particular way of seeing Midwest topography. Or the harsh surfaces of past + present—synthesized in the throaty music of the restless urban moment.

B: Listening to Susan Howe's reading live from DIA via a cell phone. Barely audible but it's a thoughtful gesture from my partner. Watched *Before the Revolution*, a **1964** Bertolucci film at Anthology Archives. A friend, Allen Midgette, is the one doing bicycle tricks in the opening. The ticket seller warns that it's a DVD version, not film. No projector smell (oily and industrial) in the auditorium. Other movies seen this winter: *Holy Motors*, *Silver Linings Playbook*, *Searching for Sugar Man*, *Detropia*, *Deep Blue Sea*, *Two Years at Sea*, *Invasion of the Body Snatchers* (**1970**s version).

G: Home from junket west, in bed with cold. Noticing *Céline and Julie Go Boating* is playing. Its palindrome shape, one girl chasing the other, then the reverse, difficult, I think, in writing prose. But loving that narrative, driving forward, suddenly reversing in the middle like a Kathy Acker sentence = a rupture which can make the writing seem angry + violent. Unreasonable. Dodie Bellamy also does this wonderfully, though her sentence structures are different, kind of end to end. As in *Cunt Norton*. The lack of a critical milieu for experimental prose means it gets read as poetry. Or else gets reviewed as conventional fiction [oft seen as ungraspable]. IF this kind of prose can do some things that poetry does, it can also do some things poetry does not. One cannot be read exactly like the other.

B: Someone I knew back in graduate school said that all of her paintings were of grids because she spent her early childhood looking through a screen door at the outside world. . . . . . . I liken my process of writing to pulling bricks out of the mud. That it is a messy struggle to discover the subject of my gaze. Reading essays, written by friends + strangers, from *Not a Rose* by Heide Hatry, on her flowers sculptured from slaughterhouse trimmings.

G: Brenda's bricks-out-of-mud corresponds with my procedural notion of peeling onion skins, recomposing until the writing intersects with the present, making a figure, perhaps a pattern that bleeds into space + time. This raises the question of who speaks when 'one' speaks? Challenging old saw of fiction POV. Brenda writes that she is trying to free herself from the sense-making demands of this world. I note that filling out an (un)employment insurance form requires 'making sense' of time spent doing art [for purposes of the form = nothing]. My flight from a brief career in journalism into a prosy/poetry space was a flight from prefabricated meaning. Journalism made me aware that certain forms, constraints, impose limited communication: width of the news column, limited acceptable vocabulary, lack of control over placement + titles. On the other hand journalism taught me to make sentences packed with subterranean meaning in resistance to teleological expectations.

B: Eating at Mile End sandwich shop, an NYC Montréal-style Jewish deli that just opened, bringing poutine, aged Québec cheddar, duck pastrami to town. Jokes about Mile High club distort the sandwich shop's name, the French and Jewish, 2 major ethnic groups of Montréal, trying to maintain their culture in an Anglo Canada. Schwartz's smoked meats. Sandwiches drenched in duck fat could produce farts. Recall maple syrup shack outside the metro station in Montréal. Fat and sugar make a potent fuel for farting.

Railroad flat? I live in a 4-room tenement apartment, built in 1900. Railroad style, that is one room opens into another, not "boxed rooms." The bathtub is not in the kitchen. The toilet is not in a closet. The rent is sky high.

G: I'll take Schwartz's in Montréal with its incredible smoked meat (fat *or* lean), dill pickles in brine, homemade fries, over that place in Manhattan. No poutine, though, with its cheese curd + meat gravy, in the iconic Schwartz family business on the Main, founded by Romanian Jewish immigrants 8 decades back. Well, none up until now. Poutine being anything but kosher—but it is true that Schwartz's was sold for a time. To a franchise partly owned by singer Céline Dion.

B: Writing from a farmhouse in Southern Indiana. Thinking about this house as a character, an actor in a poem or fiction. This house, hundred and fifty years old, ceiling falling in, my brother plans to tear it down once my mother passes away. Farm houses here are endangered. Likewise the Merry Widow, the lone tree in a field left there to shade mules or a farmer. The 2 that I always adored for their massive trunks lay in splinters, rotted by time or uprooted by a farmer for space to grow a few more bushels of beans or corn.

G: Brenda's houses + mine are not the same. But when Brenda read from *The Marvelous Bones of Time* at Université de Montréal, language roiled from land and from time in a way eerily familiar. It is hard to explain correspondences. I do know that as women who did not grow up in the intense cities we now inhabit, we are porous, have weak defences to the sensory overload of crowded conglomerations. When I am in Manhattan, Brenda's eye for detail leads me on little jaunts toward varied eccentricities, the oddest + best cafés + little hole-in-the-wall shops and writerly landmarks. The word "correspondence" takes me to Baudelaire's poem of the same name—about correspondences between "man" + nature. Weirdly or wonderfully, Baud implies that it is nature that watches "man." That's how it felt when Hurricane Sandy hit. And that's how it feels in bed on a gray day in Mile-End, the sparrows singing off-tune in the courtyard tree, which my Marxist neighbour wanted to cut because it interfered with her clothesline. Another snowstorm coming from the American Midwest, where Brenda is as I write. Shouldn't snow be coming from farther north?

B: Cardinal at the feeder, the official Indiana state bird. Local obituary of "a twenty-five-year-old . . . lost his battle with alcohol and chose to leave this life. . . ."

CODA [11/16]

D.A.M.N.A.T.I.O.N.

In . . . wild thinning of the afterwords. Election week a Gothic novel.   Gladman
Night after night. People wandering about you. In front of you.
In fog. Empty. Wolfish. Straining to grasp meaning of what, days
earlier, unfathomable. The brumey Manhattan November
ramblers. Conjuring Béla Tarr's Soviet Goth Prowler. Stalking,
drenched in drizzle. Putative end of era. "Is neo-fascism
imminent?" You asking ex-lefty bf. "Not *yet*," he chiding. "Certain
objective conditions lacking." Plus—>this not your country.
[Cozy photo of glossy Liberal leader, snow falling gently outside
window.] Still. Paler version of whatever happening here. Oft
drifting North. Then

Tonight. Walking up from bridge. Finding self threading narrow
passage. Under dim old-style New York Zinc Bar lighting. Past
row of stools. And down little steps. To be huddling. Nursing
carafon. With 2 older poets. And diverse group of youngers. From
stage, young woman's light voice saying: "IN HERE I FEEL SAFE."
To mostly empty tables. Bulk of Segue Series habituals being out.
Marching. Miles + miles of placards. Crying in dark: *NOT MY*
PRESIDENT. With outgoing Obama. In heads of many, floating

over. Gazing back like Klee's angel. While Time blowing elsewhere.

The young woman's *SAFE*. Hanging long time in air. You pouring another glass. Surprised it jolting you like that. Had things already come so far? Were not you [ex-journalist] well apprised of facts? Or was your outsider status mitigating woman's apprehension? Hours [years?] later. Dead poet sussuring in ear . . . *The old masters understood* . . . Someone always *suffering*. . . . While *someone else is eating or looking out a window*. . . . And it occurring that, like poet's *someone* in window: Head stuck in frame. Too absorbed in discombobulating clown-parade of present. To place woman's particular un-*SAFE* on continuum of monstrously homicidal continental history. But what, in interim. Between event + remembrance of it. Soliciting *face* in window. To be conjoining nether regions. Where empathy is germed. Allowing thinnest spire of illumination. To pierce the fog?

W. H. Auden

Now. Even weather. In tales of Goth heroics. Can be duplicitous: One foggy layer laid upon another. Concealing some seedy mystery. Or hidden motive. Mercifully—*such* a nice [faded] blue sky. On arriving once more. LaGuardia. On day of épormyable **2016** US elections. Nonchalant, almost. Settling in back of airport taxi. Mostly hungry. Voracious. For mundane pleasures of city. In wake of 2-year mind-blowing concussion. When cabbie. Turning onto street called Clinton. Saying: "Hillary will win." But

Air. Already heavier. Grittier. Squeezing into Wall St up-elevator. Mid several high-level pro-Hillary media mavens. Scented arms cradling champagne. Elegant tunics falling over black—or exquisitely patterned—leggings. Heels extending already skinny New York silhouettes. [Mother's mantra: *There comes a time. When a woman must choose. Between her face + her waist.*] Alas, party. No sooner starting. Friendly greetings. Happy expectant faces. Leaning. In stupendous high of emotion. Over cortèges of shapely bottles. Cheeses. Caviar. Prosciutto. Increasingly trying to ignore wide-screen TV. Flashing insulting Hillary returns. While large male journalist [crushing sofa cushions]. Pleading: *Wait! Just WAIT. Till Florida*.......... Then abruptly. It Oo-ver.

Quietly [who invited you?]. You closing condo door. Glimpsing outside 24th-floor window. Giant stars + stripes. Stretched over iconic Stock Exchange columns. [Hugeness always scaring you a little.] Mercifully, in down elevator. Sole [distressingly rosy] young woman. Holding beautiful still-wrapped flowers. Tiny faces peering knowingly through cellophane. Sweating discretely. Causing little frisson. So that

Stepping into thickly-misted street. Faces white. In passim. Shrouded, almost. Against paleness of Stock Exchange columns. One [superb camel coat] open-mouthed. Aghast to be prosperous centrist Dem [you venturing]. Ghosted in own neo-liberal nest.

Crossing square. The footfalls, silent. Stunned. Shamed to be of country. Voting in cheap reality TV star. Who already. In launching campaign. From gold escalator [no less]. Performing with little pink mouth [glittery white teeth]. Hateful stoking of right-wing hysterics. Re: alleged *druggy, thieving, rapist* Mexicans. Sneaking into guileless America. Another night

Corner, E 4th. Darker, grittier than ever. [November, heading toward solstice.] K, dark stockings, coat. Cool chunky black shoes. Stepping hazardously into traffic. To greet. You hugging. Comforting each other. In tiny mostly candle-lit bar. Over drinks. You trolling photo. Of new President-elect. Hulk-like in business suit. Torqued forward, uncomfortably to left. To get slimming photo angle. Background: glittering golden wall. Top one per cent won't care. He's messaging to them: *I'm your man*. You laughing. Appalled. Fascinated. A little.

*

Back. On Zinc Bar stage. Young woman's *Safe* still hanging in air. In wake of New Orleans poet. Whose doubly menaced queer/ black *Boy with Thorn*. Acquiring carnal knowledge. Against background of impenetrable indigo nights. Nights swathed in blue herons. Swamp lilies. Moonlight . . . *opening like a kiss*. Elements— in poet's words—of stereotypical/discursively made-up South. *Swinging / On its Gothic hinges, making the light fussier as it swags.*

While history's horrors [... *two men / Burning at edge of a field*].
Spooling out behind.

Rickey
Laurentiis

Afterwards. You recalling Zinc Bar reading. As magnificent ode to black mothers. Even raising, in lauding, to crest of reminiscence. Till coming upon scratchy event recording. And discerning no mothers.... They figuring, rather. Scant. Intense. On printed pages. Of *Boy with Thorn* volume.... *I have,* writing the poet,..... *to find the mother whose snot / And crying now constitute her son / The boy she nursed in her own arms, kissed / And sung to "Hushaby".* ...

Here, your memory again. Trying to control narrative. With its tergiversations. Creations of dislocated scenarios. For reasons oft entangled to point of unfathomable. But—as language has also made plain ... *memory is not an instrument for exploring the past, but rather a medium ... based in experience.* Indeed, in very act of looking back. We expressing [and to express is to imply an Other]. Some future [im]perfect [perhaps identitary?] desire. For the humans without boundaries we will have been. Becoming. Marcel Proust thought this. Who, in searching for Lost Time. Inventing purposefully indeterminate, meandering sentences. Sparking thinking in multiple, contrapuntal directions. Mirroring poetry. Whose formally ajar enjambments. Likewise offering space for affect + excess. De rigueur notably during moments of intense

Benjamin

social change. In its way of glomming one poet's syllables to another's—+ to the body of the reader. Poetry excelling in making micro-communities. It cannot make a revolution. It can, however, create space. For freely imagining. Edges. Of le possible.

[But you will always write in sentences.]

ACKNOWLEDGMENTS

A wide deep thanks to those Downtown Manhattan poets who befriended me at a time (the effervescent early Obama years) when the winds were blowing rather stiffly centre-right in Canada under the auspices of the Prime Minister I call Mr. SHHH herein. In my eternal quest to learn from poetry how to write better prose, I was drawn by the openness, curiosity, and conviction of the many for whom the necessary relationship between art and politics is a matter of form. It was marvellous to shove off from various city lodgings and race toward the Bowery for multiple weekly readings at iconic Downtown poetry sites. Thanks to indefatigable poet/directors James Sherry (long-standing director of the Segue Series), Stacy Szymaszek (Poetry Project director, 2007–2018), Rachel Levitsky (founder of the Belladonna* Collaborative), and Bob Holman (Bowery Poetry Club). And to their teams.

Special thanks to those who read draft sections of this memoir, for their helpful commentary, and for the prized stamp their writing has left on my work, including: Brenda Coultas, Bob Glück, Eileen Myles, John Keene, Lee Ann Brown, Carla Harryman, Tisa Bryant, Renee Gladman, and Charles Bernstein. Robbie Schwartzwald, Caroline Brown, WM Burton, and Amelia Schönbek also offered helpful commentary. Thanks to Rachel Levitsky, for ingenious conversation, and poetry, from my earliest New York visits to the present. Without Rachel this book would be something else entirely. Eileen Myles also crucially shared their queer

Manhattan in person and in their powerful writing. Poets Stacy Szymaszek, Kim Rosenfield, Abigail Child, erica kaufman, and Rob Fitterman were [and are] brilliant Downtown interlocutors. Akilah Oliver is here in luminous spirit. Brenda Coultas's New York poetry threads, notably, the reciprocal 3rd person interview in the "Gail + Brenda Go Boating" section of this book. Huge thanks also to Julie Patton for her rendering of everyday life as sublime performance art—even her e-mails are poetry. Deep thanks, also, to the fine poets Rachel Zolf, Rickey Laurentiis, and all the talented others, who by happenstance, pass more briefly than I would like across this set. Finally, I wish to note the impact of Marjorie Welish's writing and thinking on the formal issues that underscore *Furniture Music*.

I cannot say enough how much I have appreciated working with Wave editor Heidi Broadhead, whose sensitivity, meticulousness, and keen editorial intelligence made the editing process a pleasure. Thanks also to Isabel Boutiette and Blyss Ervin, for their hard work on behalf of *Furniture Music*, as well as to Joshua Beckman, Matthew Zapruder, and publicist Catherine Bresner.

Gratitude to the *Denver Quarterly* for initial publication of the interview with Brenda Coultas. And to both Belladonna* and OEI Bild in Stockholm for publishing the "Molto Moderato" section of *Furniture Music*. And thanks to Kevin Nicholls for helpful conversation about neo-liberalism.

Finally, I would like to thank Le Conseil des arts et des lettres du Québec, for granting me their SoHo studio, which provided *Furniture Music* ground from which to start. I was fortunate to have been able to travel, at a crucial time in US politics, a well-trod Montréal artist path to New York (after the likes of Leonard Cohen, Moyra Davey, Julie Doucet, to name a few). I want to acknowledge as well my inimitable hometown, Montréal, where historic French/English language struggles foster (and sometimes force!) an ongoing reflection about what it means to write across boundaries of all kinds. I am always happy to return.